Many thanks to my husband and family for providing me with their unending support and inspiring me to become what I've always wanted to be. I just needed a little guidance and a big push.

The Nine Lives of Clemenza

A Novel
By Holly Christine

The Beginning

Heaven

Clemenza started out as we all do. Billions of miles away from Earth. Just outside of the universe. In heaven. There are millions of people who debate and philosophize religion, but its actually really simple. Our universe is gigantic. And full of energies. Just outside of the universe is heaven. You can never see it until you are there and you can never imagine what it is actually like until you are there. And God created all of the energies in our universe. He created the energies and then let them roam. He has given each ball of energy the ability to choose its own destination. This is the choice that we have. And sometimes we make mistakes. So, because of these mistakes, we get a few chances. Nine, to be exact.

She waited patiently in line as we all do, waiting to meet her Maker and waiting to meet her fate. She was faceless then. Just one body of energy. No legs, no arms. She had no distinct characteristics of any being, because she wasn't one yet. Only a voice and a mind that allowed her to make choices. She was only her self, her soul. This was her first time in line to meet God.

Waiting in line in heaven is just like waiting in line for anything else, but much, much faster. God sees millions of His creations a day, all around the clock, and helps all of them with their choices. It's a line with white velvet ropes on each side, though no one would dare to jump line. No one could possibly be that impatient. There is no real, solid floor; only a white powdery substance that a smart Angel threw down so that those with a fear of heights could handle the view.

And what an amazing view. Those bored in line could watch the distant planets and stars spinning, some in control, some very out of control. They could see the stars beginning and the stars ending. Black holes, quite a spectacular sight to see, were enveloping everything around it. More energies were popping up at the end of the line every few seconds.

The two in front of her were more experienced. Clemenza could tell that they had already had a life or two. One was some sort of reptile from Earth, and the other was a microorganism from another planet... the one that God was still experimenting with. The microorganism named himself Sally. When he introduced himself as Sally, Clemenza asked, "Isn't that a female name?" to which Sally replied, "There is no such thing. You *must* be new."

Sally was complaining and that is also how Clemenza knew he was experienced. Sally said that God had better hurry up with his plans for the other planets. He said that God was playing favorites with Earth, that all of the other planets were suffering because of this favoritism.

"Do you know how many organisms exists on Earth, Clemenza?" Sally asked.

She was dumbfounded. Didn't they already establish that Clemenza was new? How would she know anything yet? If Clemenza had a mouth, it would be opened, jaw dropped. But she didn't yet. Before Clemenza could get a word in, Sally continued.

"Billions. Not even a million are on Mars, and he burned up the Sun. He made the Earth green. He made it smell wonderful. He gave it water to support life. Everyone who goes there succeeds. I have only visited once and I plan to go back this time."

The reptile cleared her throat to interrupt Sally's ranting.

"Excuse me, but what were you on Earth?" the reptile asked.

"I was a fly. I was there less than three days. I was happy, too. Flying around all over the place. Then on the third day, there I was, minding my own business, when WHACK! I flew right into a spider's web. I was eaten that night."

"Why didn't you just beg the spider to eat something else?" Clemenza asked. She thought it seemed pretty simple.

Sally laughed. "You are too young! Lemme tell you this... wherever you go, you only understand your own species. That spider had no idea what I was screaming, and good thing, too. Terrible words were coming out of my mouth. What a disappointing life! Anyway, it's only in heaven that we all understand each other. When you go to other places, you will see."

Clemenza started to create a picture of life. She knew that when it was her turn, that God would ask her what she wanted to become. God would create her into whatever she wanted, but it was up to her whether or not she would succeed. That was why everyone was given nine lives. After nine lives you could choose to retire and live in His Tenth Life Retirement Community, you could choose to go back to one of your previous lives, or you could apply to work with God as an Angel. The requirements for the position were strict, and all depended upon how you lived during your nine lives.

As she got closer to God, she could hear the infamous Angelic Harmonic Orchestra. Clemenza immediately felt inspired and beautiful. The parts that she loved the most were the deep percussion of the drums and the gorgeous melody of what Sally told her were Angel violins. Moving along the line, Clemenza stared at the Angels, with their white robes and ever changing faces. Their wings were long and thick and pointed towards the skies of heaven when they got to their own solo parts in the song that never ended. She decided then that no matter what she chose to be, in the end, she wanted to be an Angel.

"You'll get used to the noise, kid. Once you get down to wherever you're going, the music stops." Sally was trying to sound like he knew it all and was unimpressed by the sounds, but Clemenza could tell by the waiver in his voice that he too was moved by the music as they neared God.

As they neared the gate that led to the walkway that led to God's room, Clemenza asked Sally what he wanted to become now.

"I've only got three lives left, kid. And I want to be a human for all three of them. God told me the last time I was here that with my strong personality and will, I could help other planets to thrive. But I don't want to. You never know what is going to happen. I just want to be comfortable."

Clemenza watched as Sally entered the white gates and walked along the cosmic clouded path to God. Sally turned back once, or so Clemenza thought. It was hard to tell what direction a microorganism was looking.

Outside of the gates were brochures for all of the destinations you could imagine, or really what God could imagine. They were endless. He was probably the most creative guy ever. But the most popular brochure was the one on Earth. Clemenza gazed at the front cover, and wondered why Sally said that God favored Earth. The front cover was simply a picture of Earth from heaven. With its mixture of greens and blues and whites, Clemenza thought that it looked like the right place to start out.

Most of the other planets, all throughout the universe, started out the same as Earth. But a few things happened that made the planet so inhabitable. The first was its position to the Sun. Not too hot, not too cold. It also had water, to support life. Earth also possessed a singular, loyal moon, which created the seasons and the tides. It wasn't that God favored Earth, things just worked out there. In the beginning, He had imagined little planets just like Earth everywhere throughout the universe, but it just didn't happen. Because he gives everyone this freedom, to do as they wish during their lives, He has no control over what happens. He made everything, sure. But He can't make it any better or any worse. It's all up to us.

The second page of the brochure was an alphabetical listing of all of God's creations. Next to each creation was a number to let the reader know how many had chosen each creation. The numbers were always changing. Even as Clemenza stared at the page, the numbers increased. Down the list she saw a short three-letter creation that seemed very simple, and simple was probably the best place to start off.

When God called out for Clemenza, she heard the Angels playing the violins and when she turned back, she saw one of the angels wink at her. *Why would anyone want to leave here,* she thought, but then again, there were so many places to go, and if God created each one of them, they had to be just as good.

God was exactly what Clemenza expected. He had a long white robe just like the Angels. He had big brown tired eyes. He probably never slept. His arms were very long and his voice was very gentle. His eyebrows were gray and bushy and he had a long beard that Clemenza could see growing, just getting longer and longer and twirling around him and covering his office. By the time she was in the office, the beard had covered nearly everything.

And then he spoke. "That is because I know what you expected, and I want you to be comfortable. I am ever changing, and I am everything to everyone. But all together, we are just balls of energy, and you have just as much power, you just don't know how to use it."

With that He smiled. Clemenza was speechless. She handed Him the brochure and pointed to the word that she wanted to be.

"Air. An interesting first choice, Clemenza. The only advice I can give you is this... prepare to be amazed, violated, choked, and loved. No one will know what to do with you, and no one knows all that you do. You have chosen to be one of the most essential parts of life on Earth. Good luck. Also, when you get back, I would like for you to prepare a short speech on your life as Air. I want to know what lesson you learned. That is the only way that you can move along to the next life."

With that, his beard disappeared and his head turned bald, glasses came from somewhere, his robe became a short white jacket. Someone must have pictured God as a doctor of some sort.

Before she could say anything, she was tumbling fast to her first life.

Life One

Air

As Clemenza was transported to Earth, she gazed at the sights around her. The Sun was burning brightly to her left and after her sight adjusted to the light from the Sun, she began to see the other planets that orbited around the Milky Way galaxy. She knew that there was nothing that could prepare her for her first life. She had no idea how long her life would last, what would cause it to end, or how much control she would have over her life. The only idea that she still held was that of God. She knew that she had just left heaven, and was grateful that she still had her memory.

As she neared Earth, she wondered if she would be able to see Sally as a human. She wondered what Sally's face would look like and if his face would match one of the

Angel's many faces that played the violin in heaven. She hoped that Sally's human life was going well.

Suddenly, when she thought she was just about to hit Earth with tremendous force, her ride ended. Here she sat, jammed up against millions of others. She screamed out, but no one could hear her. To her right was a translucent ball that was mumbling something to the ball next to it. *They must be the same kind.* Clemenza remembered Sally saying heaven was the only place that had a universal language. Even though she was stuffed into what seemed like a tiny room, she could still see the Earth because everyone up here was clear. No one had eyes or noses or mouths or even colors to distinguish them. Clemenza could only tell that they weren't the same as her because of their language. If she didn't understand it, she knew they were different.

She sat high in the sky, in the atmosphere of Earth. Jets flew past underneath her. The stars could still be seen above her. This was a crowded place. Everyone was so packed, and it seemed as if the temperature was rising by the second. Being so small, Clemenza was easily affected by the temperature. And everyone seemed miserable. Even though she couldn't understand them, she could still tell that the tones of their voices were angry. Maybe they just had a louder language. Maybe they were all hard of hearing. Maybe they all hated each other.

It didn't take her too long to start feeling lonely. She passed the time between these other beings that complained a lot and didn't know her. They didn't even want to know her. What a life she had chosen! The one deciding factor in her choosing to become air was reading that it was essential to life. Thinking back to the brochure that she held onto so tightly during her meeting with God, she thought about her environment. She knew that air was made up of certain elements. There was oxygen, nitrogen, argon and some carbon. She recalled reading that air was made up of nearly 78% nitrogen, and because she didn't recognize the voices mumbling around her and because it sounded as if they were speaking to each other, she decided that they must be nitrogen gases.

The second most popular gas that made up the air of Earth was oxygen, about 20%. I must find out what I am, Clemenza thought. So she started screaming.

"Oxygen! Oxygen! I'm Oxygen! Is there anyone out there?"

To Clemenza's dismay, no one answered, but the nitrogen gases around her started mumbling even louder. She started thinking about how wonderful it was in heaven.

How wonderful that everyone spoke the same language, and how wonderful it felt when an Angel looked at you, making your entire soul shiver. Angels not only spoke the universal language, they felt it. So an Angel could tell what you were thinking just by being near you.

No matter what life I live, Clemenza thought, *I want to be an Angel in the end.*

Clemenza thought back to the beautiful sounds of the Angelic Harmonic Orchestra and the sounds of that one special violin, and hearing that violin, she held her breath. When she exhaled, she found herself sliding between the nitrogen gases and heard more mumbling. Finally! A way to find more Oxygen gases! She exhaled again and again, screaming, *Oxygen! Oxygen! Oxygen*! All the while she was falling closer and closer to Earth when she finally heard a voice that she could understand.

"Oxygen here, kiddo! Stay put and quit breathing so heavy! You'll fall straight to the ground with all your yelling!"

Clemenza was so relieved, she would cry if she had tear ducts.

"Oh thank you thank you thank you! I feel like I've been yelling forever. I'm Clemenza and this is my first life. Where are we?"

The Oxygen gas next to her sighed. "My name is Marilyn, and this is my fourth life. Right now we are in the Mesosphere, and I have been here for nearly ten years now."

"It is wonderful to meet you, Marilyn."

Clemenza was still a little out of breath from all of the yelling, but she had so many questions. After all, when she reported back to God after this life, she wanted to have a great lesson to share with Him so that he would grant her an even better next life.

"Why do you stay here? Don't you want to go down to Earth and see the humans?" Clemenza spoke eagerly and earnestly. She wasn't sure how long her life would last here. She had to know as much as possible as soon as possible. And she was just so excited to talk to someone.

"For us, being Oxygen, humans and other things on Earth mean the end to this life. They use us to live; they breathe us in and then *poof!* Back to God we go! But I stay here for the view. Look above you."

Clemenza leaned her head back to see the most amazing sight, even more beautiful than the burning Sun, the twirling planets, the flight to Earth. Marilyn called it the Northern Lights. It danced around in the sky above them with such grace and such meaning and as Clemenza watched the colors moving around, she realized that they were dancing to the Angels' music from heaven. And now, for the first time since she left heaven, she smiled. She looked to her side and saw Marilyn smiling, too.

Clemenza enjoyed Marilyn's company because she told great stories from her past lives. She said that she used to be an actress when she was a human and that her acting ability was the sole reason she was a great storyteller. When Clemenza asked her questions, she always answered, but Marilyn's voice always grew a little slower and a little sadder when she spoke of her time as a human. She said that she struggled with sadness in all of her lives, and that being Oxygen was one of the only things that truly made her happy.

"Those lights make me feel like I'm in heaven, and yet here I am, as close to Earth as I can be without dying." Marilyn kept her body tilted back when she spoke, as if seeing the lights was her only way of speaking.

"I was so sad on Earth that I hated myself," she continued. "Can you imagine? Hating your own life, being that miserable? I mean, I tried to lead the best life that I could, I just didn't know how to do it. I didn't believe in God. I didn't believe in heaven and I already thought that I was in hell, which doesn't exist, by the way. God just lets the bad ones go by having one last life. Then they just die. Their soul dies. I don't now why He chose to let me stay. He let me pick another life. I think that He saw that it was sadness, not evil that made me bad."

Now, Clemenza was trying to listen to everything that Marilyn said, but after she said that she didn't believe in God when she was a human, Clemenza was a little stumped.

"How did you not believe when you had already met Him?" Clemenza asked.

"Because God doesn't let humans remember their past lives. When you are human, you are born with a blank mind. You have no memories. You simply don't remember God. I forgot that He existed. And as my life as a human became worse and worse, I simply couldn't believe that there was a God that would allow such terrible things to happen to me. I was a little selfish, I suppose. Now I am just a spectator to life. I watch. I don't participate. And I am happy with that."

Clemenza sat in silence and contemplated the thought of not knowing God as they watched the lights dance in the sky to the music of Angels. She couldn't imagine forgetting anything. So far in her life she knew three things, and God was one of them. The other two were

Sally and Marilyn. And then Clemenza thought about how happy Sally was to go back to his life as a human. She remembered that Sally wished to live all of his last lives as a human. How could two beings think so differently if we were all made the same? And that was when she realized that we all had one thing in common: We have the freedom to choose what we want. We choose what we want to be and we choose what we do once we become what we are.

Marilyn gazed above as the dancing lights slowly came to an end. She told Clemenza about her life as a human and the obstacles that she had to overcome in her human life. She said it was the hardest of all the lives that she had. She was born into a very large and very poor family. Her father couldn't read, but he still went to work every morning to support his family. Her mother raised all five girls nearly by herself, because by the time her father got home, he was too exhausted to even say a single word. Her mother told her that it was because of his exposure to war at a young age, but Marilyn knew that when she looked into her father's eyes she saw her own, and that they were both full of sadness, that war had nothing to do with it.

"What war? What is war?" Clemenza had so much to learn.

Marilyn continued. She said that the humans had divided the Earth into countries, and when countries disagreed with each other, they went to war. *No, not to talk things over. To take over.* If one country has something that the other wants, they will go to war to either protect that thing or to conquer it. *No, they don't share.* How do you determine the winner? Well, the country with the most men standing at the end generally wins. *No, the others don't sit.* They all lay dead on the ground. Humans are the only living things that kill their own kind.

"Do you think that maybe because humans aren't born with the memory of heaven, that maybe since they don't remember, they have no idea what happens after their life ends, is that why they kill each other?"

Marilyn said that yes, perhaps, maybe that was the reason why humans killed other humans. And maybe that was the reason why they worked so hard for a job that means nothing in the end; maybe that was why they forgot about their own family, why they cared more about money (something that doesn't even really exist, humans made it) than their family and friends. Clemenza listened intently, but knew that she could not take everything Marilyn said to heart. Marilyn was clearly a sad being, and it made

Clemenza sad that Marilyn could not see beyond her own sadness.

"When I am a human, I won't forget. I will care for everyone around me, so that I can learn my lesson and then maybe God will let be become an Angel."

Marilyn smiled at the thought of Clemenza's ignorance. She said, "You won't remember once you get there, but it doesn't hurt to try."

Below them, a weather balloon struggled to predict unpredictable weather, and above them, the Northern lights danced effortlessly. This was a restful place, now, with Marilyn sharing it with her. For a while, when Marilyn and Clemenza spoke, no other noise was heard. But as time passed, there was more and more noise around them. It wasn't quite the language of nitrogen. It was something new.

Although Clemenza and Marilyn were constantly moving, they tried their best to stay together. Occasionally, they would not see each other for some periods of time, though time was not something that was real to them. The only way to mark time was by noting the moments they were together and the moments they were apart. Because they moved about, they met other Oxygens and Marilyn was starting to pick up on some of Nitrogen's language. The next time the pair met, Marilyn had news.

"So I found out that the others that we have been seeing more of are actually called Carbons. They are coming from Earth. Apparently, humans are burning more fossil fuels, and Carbons are released from the burning. In conclusion, I will never become a fossil fuel. It would be a very short life nowadays." Marilyn still had that dazed expression.

Clemenza wondered why Marilyn carried all of her sadness with her. She wouldn't let it go, just kept holding onto it, letting it take the blame for everything that happened. It was her eternal excuse. Sadness.

She said she never wanted to have a life that was shorter than her human life. The Carbons normally left the atmosphere, but because there were more and more of them, it was taking more time for them to leave. And now Clemenza was hearing them more and more. And it sounded like they were complaining, too.

As Clemenza spent more and more time as Oxygen, she realized that she wasn't learning any lessons. Her days were the same. There was nothing to learn here. She decided that she needed to get closer to other types of life to learn anything. Though it saddened her to leave Marilyn and the sights of the Northern lights, she knew that she could always come back. If she wanted to, she could find Marilyn once she retired. There were lessons to be learned, and apart from learning about the atmosphere and sad Marilyn, she learned nothing about her self. She was eager to move on.

She started allowing herself to fall. The further she fell, the more she learned. Planes zoomed past her, and for the first time, Clemenza saw a human face. The plane was flying through the clouds, and Clemenza was keeping up with it. In the window she saw a human child's face. She couldn't stop watching. The child gazed out the window, and was watching Clemenza as she kept pace with the plane.

She wondered if the child could see her, but she knew she was invisible, but still. The child never looked away from her. As the plane finally neared the ground, she watched the child grab his stuffed toy dog. He listened as the child spoke an unknown language to his mother. The child reached for his mother's arms and as she lifted him, the child turned to Clemenza and smiled.

Marilyn was miles and miles above, and for some reason, Clemenza suspected that Marilyn must have once felt what that child was feeling. Clemenza wanted to know what it felt like. She wanted to know what it felt like to be held, to be lifted into the arms of a mother. Clemenza knew no such thing. She started to climb higher into the air, but never lost eye contact with the child.

Finding another Oxygen, she spread the word to find Marilyn and ask her to come to this spot.

When Marilyn arrived, she saw the eye contact that the child was still keeping with Clemenza.

"He can't see you, Clemenza, that would be impossible. But I do wonder what he is staring at, huh? He does look like he sees you. Move around. Let's see if his eyes move with you."

Marilyn watched in amazement as the child's eyes followed Clemenza, left and right, up and down. He was still smiling, too. Throwing the toy dog up in the air, looking as if he were trying to hit Clemenza with it. Maybe knock her down, bring her home, and keep her in a glass jar, and every human that would see it would say "Hey, kid, that's a nice jar of nothing" not even knowing that Clemenza was in there.

"Is it possible for the boy to feel me?" Clemenza asked. She felt a rush of excitement of the possibility of someone else besides an Oxygen particle seeing her.

"If you drop a little lower, maybe catch the wind, you may be able to breeze past his face. But be careful," she warned. "If you get too close he may breath you in."

Before another word could be said, Clemenza was dropping, caught the wind, and drifted across the boy's face. The boy smiled and began to laugh. Clemenza laughed, too. It was the first time she ever felt joy. She felt joy in being recognized by another and she felt joy herself by making the boy laugh. She decided that she wanted to see the boy grow up, to watch what a human life was like before she experienced it. That way, when she became a human, she would know how to have the best life she could.

"I am sad to leave you, Marilyn, but I think it is time. I have lessons to learn, huh? This is the only way to do it."

And that day Marilyn watched as Clemenza, surely one of the nicest, but one of the most naive souls she had ever met, left her. She watched as Clemenza dropped closer to Earth, just clinging to the particles of the air behind the boy's head so that he couldn't breathe her in. She felt inspired by Clemenza's eagerness, but knew that she wasn't ready to be eager yet. She was ready to return to the sky and watch her lights.

Clemenza watched him grow. And it was a tough life on Earth for Clemenza. Strong winds blew her around and sometimes right near the faces of unknown humans. She had close calls with death, each and every day. And Clemenza had days now. She noted that when the sun lit the Earth, the humans lit up, too. They lit up with life. She watched the boy's mother and father leave for work everyday. She watched the boy catch the bus every morning for school. She caught the wind and watched him through the window of the bus, just as she watched him for the first time on the plane. And he watched her back. Wherever he was looking, Clemenza was always there. She was there when his parents were screaming at each other downstairs. She was there to watch him cry himself to sleep and sometimes gasp for breath between his cries.

As she watched him grow, she learned a few human words. The boy's name was Christopher. This was the name he responded to when his mother or father or teacher or classmate called it out. But not everyone called him Christopher. The kids in his classroom had other names that Christopher didn't respond to. When they called him these names, she watched him draw in his notebook, as if he weren't paying any attention to them at all, but she knew that he was. She knew that he was bothered by it. Clemenza was there when the kids from his class threw their food at him in the lunchroom, and followed him to the bathroom when he felt like crying.

Occasionally, Marilyn would come down and watch with Clemenza. Marilyn would say that the boy had the same sadness that she did. Sometimes she would have to leave because watching the boy cry made her remember when she was a young girl. She said that she had cried enough tears as a human, and would leave to watch the high skies perform.

Marilyn left for years and Clemenza sometimes wondered if she should leave the boy alone. She was getting tired of the boy never defending himself in school. Christopher was just letting his life pass him by, just like Marilyn. But soon enough, that would all change. It was nighttime and Clemenza was flying in the breeze of the window air conditioner. She was watching the clock on the nightstand, when Christopher abruptly sat straight up in bed. He was gasping again, but this time he wasn't crying. He was holding his chest and gasping for air, for something.

Clemenza knew now why she had waited and watched him all of this time. She called out for help, and millions of Oxygen particles came tumbling from above. As a group, they approached Christopher's wide-open mouth, closed their eyes and went in. And that was the end.

Back in line, Clemenza had completed her first life. In front of her was Marilyn, who had helped to give Christopher the breath of air that his body needed to live.

They found out from the Angels that Christopher was diagnosed with asthma and the night they died, they gave Christopher the oxygen that his body needed in order to survive. Because of this incident, Christopher's parents took him to the doctor who then gave Christopher an inhaler. Clemenza was grateful that Christopher had something to replace her on Earth. And now she knew what she needed to tell God in order to move on to her next life.

When her name was called she marched through the gates of God's office with the same smile on her face that she had when she first made Christopher laugh.

God looked different this time. Maybe it was from all of the jets that flew past her in the sky. But he was wearing a pilot's uniform this time and He didn't look happy about it. The Angels on the outside of the gates were smirking a bit when Clemenza walked in.

"And what lesson have you learned during your life as air?" God got right to the point. Maybe he wanted to hurry up and get this over with, wearing that silly captain's hat and all.

"I learned that I had a purpose. My purpose as air was to save the life of Christopher."

"And how do you feel about what you did, Clemenza?" He tipped the corner of his hat up, revealing his blue eyes now to match his blue uniform and adjusted the name tag on his freshly pressed shirt. God.

"I feel wonderful." Clemenza was still smiling. "Next, I want to be the Northern Lights."

The second that Marilyn told Clemenza that she wanted to be air for the rest of her life so that she could always watch the Northern Lights, Clemenza had decided that that was what she wanted to be. Marilyn had helped her save Christopher, and now Clemenza would have a chance to do something to make Marilyn happy.

God informed her that it was a tough life to choose, but that he had confidence in her. He was impressed by her courage and selflessness as Oxygen. And then she was tumbling through the universe again.

Life Two
The Northern Lights

And just like that, Clemenza's second life began. She
was quickly taken directly to the Sun, which she
thought was a huge mistake. Maybe God misunderstood
her. Did she say the Northern Lights? Maybe she was too
cocky. She was on such a rush from saving Christopher's
life. Maybe this was God's way of putting her in her place...
sending her to a place that was hot as hell. Clemenza
doubted that she would meet anyone here. How could
anyone survive?

The Sun was a gigantic, bubbly mess. On arrival,
Clemenza was grateful to meet her first second life
acquaintance. His name was Solare, which he promptly told
Clemenza was Italian for Solar, if Clemenza even knew
where Italy was. That's what he said. Clemenza told him
that her name was Clemenza which was Italian for

Clemenza, and putting together what his name meant was pretty much common sense. She didn't want him to think he could bully her, but bullying appeared to be his job.

Solare rolled his eyes and handed Clemenza a pamphlet of fire that she was to read and memorize by the next day. When she asked him when the next day was he said now. She had already failed the first test. Everything moves quickly on the Sun.

"I'll just sum everything up for you, okay? Since you are completely incapable of reading the pamphlet that I spent years perfecting. Years. Not that I would expect you to understand, okay? Just listen, okay?"

"Okay."

"Okay."

There was an awkward pause in their battle to have the last word. The Sun had just spit up and now what was part of the Sun was heading towards Venus to destroy whatever was there. Clemenza just hoped that no one she knew was there. Not that she knew many people. Even her thoughts moved quickly on the Sun.

"Okay." Solare did have the last word. In fact, he had double the last word. Clemenza thought that Solare was in competition even with himself.

"The Sun is the reason that we even have a working galaxy here, okay? Because of the Sun, we have enough gravity to pull the planets into an orbit. Because of her sheer size, we have a galaxy, okay? Just lemme know when you get lost here, okay? Am I talking too fast for you? Okay. So the Sun is the reason for life. But not exactly the reason, she just makes life more possible, okay? The Sun is the reason the Earth, which by the way was voted most popular planet in the annual Cosmos survey, has seasons. The Sun is the reason why humans wake up and fall asleep. The Sun is the God of the people who don't believe in God."

Clemenza listened to Solare's words but still didn't know why she was here.

"I was supposed to be the Northern Lights."

Solare sighed. "You will be. Okay? But you have to know everything first. You just can't go in there without knowing anything. You'll mess it up for everyone. You might even kill people. Okay? This is no joke. It's not romantic. It's your job."

Clemenza found out that she would first be attending dance classes. And not just by anyone, but by Aurora Borealis herself. She invented the movement. That was why everything had to be perfect. Aurora had been alive for millions of years. This was still her first life. And she was making the most of every moment of it. While waiting in line, again, to enter the dance classroom, Clemenza overheard that Aurora was ready to retire. She was looking for someone to replace her. Everyone behind Clemenza was hoping that they would be the chosen one to replace her.

The Northern Lights existed because of the Sun. When the Sun burst out flares, the flares did not return. They traveled through place thousands of miles per hour and met with the Earth's atmosphere several days later. When they collided with the atmosphere, they became the Northern Lights, particles of gas spreading across the sky in beautiful colors. This was what Marilyn was always watching and Clemenza wanted to have Marilyn see her in action.

But Aurora was certainly not the nicest being that ever existed. She demanded perfection from all of her pupils. And Clemenza was learning that everything that happened and everything that was on the Sun happened very, very quickly. It would be the equivalent of having Starbucks' strength coffee instead of blood for humans.

The classroom was just like a regular ballet classroom, except it was very hot. And it was on the Sun.

Not really on the Sun, because there was not one solid surface. It was more *in* the Sun. And Aurora was perhaps one of the most beautiful things that Clemenza had ever seen. Her long gown was made of so many solar gases that it danced behind her and flowed with whatever music Aurora heard in her mind. Each step that she made was defined and intentional, never slipping, and her movements with her arms were just like the solar flares, curved, quick, and graceful. It was amazing to Clemenza that such a beautifully graceful creature could exist in such a chaotic place as the Sun. Perhaps this was the reason that so many feared Aurora. They feared her own power over her own movements.

Aurora clapped twice and music immediately began.

"The Moonlight Sonata. Adagio. Meaning. Slowly. Slowly. Starting in first. Slow sustained movements." Aurora flowed over to Clemenza and kicked her feet out further. "Toes OUT!"

Clemenza concentrated on Aurora's words, putting all of her energy into her own movements. She wanted to impress Aurora, but she had no idea what she was supposed to be doing. She had no background in ballet. She had no knowledge of the terminology. If she had been given more time, perhaps she would have read that pamphlet that Solare had given her. She had a few questions for him anyway, so she planned to search for him after her class was finished. Clemenza was also stunned by the expectation of her to make slow movements when everything around her was moving so quickly. This was going to be nearly impossible. Much, much more difficult than being air.

"Now, plie, releve." Aurora's words began to melt together in the heat of the Sun. She was all over the room at once, standing next to each of her new students at the same time. Yelling commands that each student heard, and yet no one knew who she was talking to. She then stopped and the music stopped with her. All eyes were on her.

"This is what I expect of you next time." The music started again, the Moonlight Sonata, adagio, or whatnot, and the class stared in awe and Aurora moved her body with each sound and turn of the music in the most beautiful positions, legs long, arms wide, no face, just movements. And Clemenza realized that the reason why Aurora demanded perfection was because she could feel how beautiful it would look in the end.

Over the next few days, Clemenza read over the pamphlet and had a few brief conversations with Solare. He seemed to pop up just as she got into her reading.

"The rumor is true," Solare exhaled with a sigh that could make an Angel frown. He seemed to be completely exhausted and disappointed at the same time.

"What rumor? About Aurora? Is she really resigning?"

"Not only resigning, okay? Dying. Becoming the Northern Lights is a suicide mission. You will live your short life here just perfecting the moves that you will make as you die. No one realizes how sad it is. Aurora is picking the class that she will leave the Sun with to have her final dance. I am thinking about going with her." Solare never looked so sad.

"The Sun needs you, Solare! You can't just leave. Who will replace you?"

"Well certainly not you." At least he still had his insulting demeanor about him. He couldn't be that sad. And in the end, Clemenza knew that Solare would never sacrifice his position in the Sun for someone else's glory. He simply was not yet ready.

Classes continued and the movements became trickier, more beautiful. Clemenza began to excel and Aurora began to notice. She asked Clemenza if she had ever seen the Northern Lights on Earth and Clemenza told that yes, she had. *Were they beautiful?* Clemenza told her the lights were the most beautiful thing she saw on Earth and that it was an honor to be a part of the movement.

"I am thinking about going. I have done this for so long and have never had the privilege of seeing what I have created with my own eyes. I have been selfless for too long." When Aurora spoke it was like a song, her words were lyrics and her body was dance. She truly was a beautiful being.

Aurora publicly announced that day that she was searching for her replacement. She would be carefully observing her classes to find someone as perfect as herself and also to find the perfect class to go out with. Clemenza hoped she would leave with her class.

Preparation for the grand event began. Aurora combined a thousand classes into one. She wanted to make the biggest and best show. A special composer who was a human in one of his last lives was brought in by Solare to create a new song for the show. Of course, the song was to be memorized by all of the thousands of dancers in the show because no music would be played during the final event. The music was simply in the souls of each dancer and Aurora herself.

The Sun was humming with songs and dances as everyone prepared. Hearts were broken when dancers discovered that they would not play a part in the show. But this was to be expected. Only the perfect could perform with Aurora. The show was to honor her life and achievements.

As it turned out, the composer that Solare had chosen was deaf in his human life, but he was now known as the greatest composer to have ever existed. And there was a terrible argument when he first arrived. As it turns out, the Moonlight Sonata was his creation, his song, and the composer who had created the music for Aurora before was taking credit for his masterpiece. After much deliberation and a trial that proved that the deaf composer was the creator of Moonlight Sonata, the phony composer was put to death by solar flare. He was expelled from the Sun and never returned. On Earth, scientists would be studying this rare gigantic solar flare expulsion for years, debating why and how it occurred; never knowing it was just one phony composer.

The composer decided on his Fifth Symphony, a piece that he had created while on Earth instead of a new piece because after witnessing the talents of the dancers and Aurora's beauty, he said that it was as if he had created the masterpiece for this last dance without ever knowing why until now.

The song started out strong and was meant to be the introduction to the green dancers. In the dance, the green dancers were plentiful and were to appear as if they were competing with the red light that was Aurora. She was the lighter note of the masterpiece. And when they collided or came near each other, the song intensified. For Aurora's solo movements, which she fully deserved, the composer played a gentle song that eventually led to the green dancers chasing her across the sky until she finally came to an end.

Multiple colors within a single dance were generally more difficult, but Aurora was creating the most difficult performance of her life. Each day the green light dancers practiced their moves, knowing they weren't nearly as stunning as the red light that Aurora would create, but complied because they were going to be a part of the greatest Northern Lights show ever seen.

Throughout all of the preparation for her final dance, Aurora had to make a few difficult decisions. Who would be her predecessor? And after days and days of practicing the dance, she realized that she needed someone else to help her with the red light. She couldn't do it herself because the conditions of Earth would make the green dancers, which were far more plentiful, the main events. Her red light would seem small, and not as important as the piece demanded she be. For this decision she had to swallow her pride and ask for help. She had to choose someone who was able to make the show, *her* show, the best and to show the importance of her performance.

The night before the dancers were to leave the Sun, Aurora made a speech. The composer also set this speech to music. He called it "Fur Aurora," although a few who had previous lives on Earth recognized the piece as "Fur Elise." The composer, after the performance, would be expelled by solar flare as well. The souls of the Sun had little patience and time for falsehoods.

"Dancers. We are about to perform the greatest show that the Earth will ever witness. Humans will talk about it for generations. We have decided on the location." She turned to her right and Solare handed her the information, which he had greatly researched, conditions of

Earth's atmosphere, time of night, etc, and nodded his head. Clemenza held back a chuckle, because she could almost hear him say "Okay."

"Fairbanks, Alaska. They will see the greatest display that we have ever given them. You were all chosen for your impeccable grace and ability. Your movements will become light in the night sky. You will be the awe and inspiration to millions. And I am honored to have you be a part of my final dance. My last performance. There is no one better. As for who will continue to teach the fine art that has come to be known as the Northern Lights, Solare is more than a leader. He is a perfectionist. And the Sun will accept him as the new instructor."

Solare smiled for the first time in his life on the Sun. He had huge shoes to fill. But he knew that he was capable. He expected Aurora to chose him. He acted surprised and humble, but to those who knew him best, he still appeared as arrogant as ever.

"I've also come to my final decision. I have done this for too long to be simple enough to assume that I can create the red lights on my own. So I must choose someone to help me. This person is selfless and I believe that she knows the importance of the perfection that is demanded of this dance."

The audience was holding its breath, awaiting Aurora's decision. Each dancer hoped that she would choose them. Each dancer waited and waited while the anticipation loomed over their heads. Even the Sun seemed to stop, not completely, that would be disastrous, but stopped just enough to add to the emotion of all that listened.

"Clemenza. I would be honored if you would dance my last dance by my side."

Clemenza simply nodded. She was too excited to say anything and too nervous to open her mouth. She wanted this to be perfect for Aurora. And Aurora nodded back as if she completely understood what Clemenza was feeling, like a mother nods at her daughter on her wedding day. It would be the last dance.

And before anyone knew it, they were shot from the Sun. It was a long trip to Earth, about two days, even at the incredible speed they were going. The green dancers stretched and practiced and hummed the music that the talented composer taught them. They didn't speak to each other. Just their presence together was enough to know the importance of what they were about to do. Some got sick. Others looked on as the Earth became closer and closer in their sight, and contemplated the ability of those who got queasy on the trip.

"Just keep your eye on the Earth" Aurora had said. Just as a ballerina keeps her eye on a point while she pirouettes to avoid dizziness. They should have listened to Aurora. A few of the sick ones eventually drifted off before they hit Earth. The pressure was too great for them.

Now they were seconds from Earth, and the dancers braced themselves for the impact, spinning and spinning and spinning, green lights now. And then Clemenza followed Aurora through her graceful and difficult movements and the composer's song came to life with light in the sky above Fairbanks, Alaska. On Earth, all that anyone could see were the gorgeous green lights and then suddenly, the red. The red danced through the green, creating curtains of light beneath her. Clemenza kept her sights only on Aurora, who was in her prime, dancing like never before. Her last dance.

The green and red lights looked on Earth as if they were competing in a race, taking over each other at certain points, racing, dripping with grace. And then a red light solo, quiet at first, then racing across the sky and taking over the green until the green ended the dance by swallowing red whole.

On Earth, only a few hundred actually witnessed the show. But one of those hundred had a video camera, and stared in disbelief as he taped the performance, jaw dropped. He would later set it to music that he felt the lights moved to. But he was wrong. There was not one being on Earth that heard Beethoven's Fifth Symphony in the movements of the lights. The lights took over the song; making it the greatest dance that Aurora had ever choreographed. Clemenza only hoped that Marilyn witnessed the performance.

At the final moment of Aurora's life, she looked back at Clemenza and smiled, her facial features suddenly revealed, and then she was gone. One nanosecond later Clemenza was, too. And they stood in line together in heaven.

They had a few moments to discuss what they where going to be. And word of the greatest light performance ever seen quickly spread through heaven. Everyone who saw Aurora congratulated her. She decided that she wanted to be a human. She wanted to see the lights through human eyes.

Clemenza wasn't sure of what she wanted to be next. It was difficult to top what she had just accomplished. She would have to speak with God and have Him guide her on her next path, her next life. When her name was called, she walked into God's office and looked around. A few things had changed. The brochures were updated. Clemenza was gone for longer than she realized.

God, a single beam of light, noticed her taking in the changes and said that he had recently acquired an Angel that was a professional organizer in her human life, and now everything was getting tidied up in heaven. Clemenza couldn't tell if He was embarrassed or excited about the changes. He was emotionless to her as he asked her what she had learned.

"It was quite a journey. I learned that it takes more than one being to make something beautiful happen. And I learned how to work with others as a team, to put aside differences. But I don't know what I want to be next."

God showed her a brochure on birds. He said that with her experience in life so far, a bird would be the next best step. "You'll love the feel of the wind beneath you. You can go anywhere."

On the cover of the brochure was a picture of a Bald Eagle, the funniest looking creature Clemenza had ever seen. After God told her that the bird was the national symbol of freedom in America, Clemenza said, "I'm ready for that."

Life Three
American Bald Eagle

The pamphlet that she read in heaven simply stated this: American Bald Eagle... symbol of freedom in United States. In fact, all of the entries for lives were short. Perhaps this was God's way of really allowing you to choose your own destiny. He didn't want to be biased. He didn't want his opinions of the creatures and beings that He created to rub off on anyone else. But He didn't really have opinions about the creatures themselves, only the souls that inhabited them.

In each life, Clemenza was unprepared for what events were to occur. But she always made the most of them. This was her first life that she would actually be able to experience the wind, the Sun from a distance, the sea. She would be able to feel each of these. And she would also experience other feelings that she had never experienced before.

The container that she was in now was very warm and filled with fluid. She seemed to be swimming in it at first and had no vision, no hearing. She only felt. As the days passed, as always, she worried that God made a mistake, He sent her to the wrong place. She seemed to be in this container forever and now her body was growing, each day getting closer and closer to the walls of the container. Soon she was sure that she would either burst her container or suffocate on her own body. Whatever was happening outside of this shell was noisy. She could feel the vibrations of two beings speaking, and knowing what she knew so far, she knew that if she could understand them, they must be the same kind as her. They must be her parents.

Throughout her days in the shell she felt warmth and sometimes coolness as her parents switched positions. During the cool phases she would start to rub at the shell with her nose, hoping that one day she could get out. Up and down up and down she rubbed her nose against the only place that she knew as home so far in this new life. And one day she felt a rubbing back. *There must be another shell against her,* she thought. A brother or a sister! A sibling she had never known before. The rubbing became a sort of language to Clemenza and her unknown sibling. When she grew weary of rubbing her nose against the shell, she would feel the vibration of a rubbing back, as if to say, *I'm still here, Where are you?*

And because of this new language, this new feeling of compassion for her unknown sibling outside of that shell, Clemenza never stopped rubbing and finally, finally a breaking! It was a small tear at first. She had weakened the shell with the rubbing and was finally getting a sense for what was outside. She felt the wind. And having been part of the wind before, she appreciated it. Knowing that tiny particles were everywhere around her, knowing that they were living lives, too. Knowing that everything was alive.

Using her nose she pushed through the small break and made a large crack that nearly ripped the shell in two. One final push and she was out. She felt a rush of wind on her head, pushing the matted hairs around twirling, dancing their own dance. Her mother immediately started screaming.

"Winston! She's here! Our first baby has pushed through the shell," she said. Clemenza's mother was slightly larger than her father. "Go out and get some more fish. And we'll need some sort of deodorizer. She stinks to high heaven. Get some conifer, too, while you're out. And hurry up. Baby two has cracked the shell."

Winston mumbled something smart back to his wife and Clemenza vaguely saw her mother's head twist to the side, trying to catch what her tired husband just said. Winston had spent nearly the entire last month gathering food for his wife, Justice. She was a demanding bride, but he loved her from the first moment he saw her. He was four years older than she and had lost his first wife during a tragic hunting accident. When his first baby was born, Winston was on his way back from collecting various twigs to make the nest a little larger. He was nearly a mile from home when he saw it happen. His baby was attempting to catch the wind and make its first flight, when it began to fall. A protective mother, Leona, his first wife, swooped to rescue the baby and was captured by a mountain lion as she neared the ground. His first child and wife dead, Winston immediately began searching for a new wife.

He met Justice during mating season, hearing only her cries for attention. She was a strong female, like Leona, and strong minded. She chose Winston and they pledged to spend their lives together. Clemenza was their first child. And a second was coming, too. It was rare for both eggs to survive. Winston felt as if some kind of guardian angel was making up for the tragedy that haunted him daily.

Officially being born, Clemenza had limited vision. Her mother helped her out of her shell and rubbed her new body as she attempted to make a few steps but failed. Her legs weren't strong enough yet. And she felt a pang that she had never experienced before. She started to scream.

"Shush, little one. Daddy's coming back soon, " Justice spoke with such calm in her voice that Clemenza stopped whining and turned her head to the side just in time to see her brother crack his shell. She could hear him rubbing the sides of the shell with such veracity that Clemenza was sure he'd knock the whole nest down.

The nest was new, too. It was Winston's masterpiece. Long before Justice laid her eggs, Winston began his work. Justice would collect small, sweet smelling twigs to make up the inner portions of the nest. Winston collected the large pieces; he made the foundation high above the ground on the Pacific coast. They had marvelous views of the sunset and could hear the waves crashing just beyond the rocky coast. After Leona was killed, this was a spot Winston frequented, lamenting the death of his wife and child. And now, it was the place of birth. A rebirth for him. A new life.

Each day, Justice and Winston weaved their new home, knowing that any day Justice would be laying her eggs. Winston wanted everything to be perfect.

He returned later in the day, just before Clemenza's brother poked through the top of his shell. When Winston landed on the nest, Clemenza jumped back. Her father's talons were gigantic and held food and conifer, just as Justice had requested. After he dropped the food and conifer, Winston carefully balled his talons together, walking on fists, not to hurt the children. Justice did the same. One hurried step could spear their children. They had heard stories.

Justice tore the fish into smaller pieces and opened her mouth, full of food, for Clemenza. Famished, Clemenza ate every piece she could manage. She felt hunger and satisfaction for the first time. Her brother was still struggling with his shell, so Clemenza lovingly nudged the shell and lay next to it. She didn't want to miss a thing.

When George, her brother, finally emerged, the family was complete.

Days passed and George and Clemenza played as their loving parents admired their creation.

"When can I fly?" Clemenza always asked. She had attempted to catch the wind a few times now, but fear and inexperience stalled her short.

"When you are ready, little one." Justice spoke in her calm yet tired voice. She had changed over the past few days. She disappeared for longer periods of time, always returning with food, but with sadness in her voice.

Winston shared her sadness. Part of having the children meant letting them go. They would raise the kids, feed them, support them, answer all of their questions, and watch them go. A few years from now the siblings would be ready to find a mate and create their own family. It was a bittersweet gift that God gave them. The joy of having created a family and the terrible feeling of loss as the children grew older, more independent.

George never asked questions. He simply did as he felt. The first day he felt like flying, he did, and his wings weren't yet strong enough to hold his awkward body and he fell. He fell so hard that he did nothing the next day. But the day after that, he tried again. Clemenza waited until Justice said she could fly. Each day she would practice, stretching her long wings wide enough to feel the wind, and quickly closing them. Just like her final dance with Aurora, she wanted everything to be perfect.

Clemenza and George grew quickly as the weeks passed. Their bodies began to fill in, looking more graceful. For the first few weeks their heads and feet were too big for their bodies, but now as they grew, Clemenza began to understand why Justice wanted her to wait to fly. Black feathers that added resistance to the wind were covering the soft tiny gray hairs that once covered their bodies. These were the feathers that would allow her to fly.

A few mornings later, Clemenza awoke to George screaming.

"Ma! Ma! I'm hungry!" he screamed.

Clemenza realized that they were alone. Justice and Winston had left them.

"Menza, wake up. Mom and Dad are gone. I watched them leave early this morning. They left together." George was worried and afraid. They had never been alone. When his parents left, he watched as Justice took a final look at her children. Winston tossed a small fish into the nest and they left. Just gone.

Clemenza looked at the remains of the fish. George had eaten nearly the whole thing, greedily, just assuming the Justice and Winston would bring his food forever. She realized that the parents left so that she and George would learn to live for themselves.

"I'm outta here." George was quick to assume he was strong enough to leave. The first fall that he had occurred even before his black feathers grew in.

Clemenza knew how long it took George to recover from that nearly fatal fall. Although she was identical to George, Clemenza knew that she was stronger, but her brother had such a hothead, he thought he could do anything. Spreading his wings, he caught the first gust of wind and vanished. Clemenza popped her head over the sides of the nest, high atop the mountains. They were so high in the trees. She watched as George seesawed through the air. He was still injured.

Seconds later, after spotting a rodent, George dove. Clemenza held her breath as she watched George plummet to the ground below. Falling was not the hard part of flying. Recovering from the fall and continuing skyward was the difficult part, as George was about to learn. He grasped the squirrel with his mighty talons and continued flying with great speed so that he could lift himself higher. Closer and closer to the ground until head over heels he fell, dislocating his right wing, still clutching the animal. He said nothing.

Clemenza spread her wings, shaking them up and down, getting her body accustomed to the movement. And then she was in the sky. She felt the wind on her wings like never before. It felt so good. She wanted to stay forever. Her body pierced the sky with each movement she made. And very slowly, she began to drop. Foot by foot, she made her way to George, still clenching the rodent.

She stood next to her broken brother.

"I will take the food up first. Then I'll be back for you." Clemenza eased the squirrel from George's talons. He reluctantly gave up the meal, once snapping at her, then painfully throwing his body back into the hard dirt.

Clemenza stretched her black body and lifted the now dead rodent into the sky with her. It was heavy on her new body, a body that wasn't even accustomed to carrying her own weight yet. Getting George was going to be the hard part. He would be devoured in minutes if she didn't save him. An injured bird on the floor of the forest was easy prey.

She quickly left and watched in horror as a wildcat slowly moved in on George. He still said nothing; ashamed of the position he put himself and his sister into. As the wildcat neared, Clemenza swooped down low beside him, distracting the cat enough to have a few seconds to lift George from the ground.

"Clench your talons, George. I will grab yours and then as I lift you will have to hold onto mine. Interlace them with mine and I will try to get you back."

George closed his eyes and clenched his talons into a ball, just as his father did when he entered their nest. And just as the wildcat as about to pounce, Clemenza grabbed his talons, lifting him into the air. He struggled to hold on, attempting to intertwine his talons with hers as she strained to lift him higher and higher to safe ground.

She did it. She saved her brother. And George was too stubborn to even thank her for it. She couldn't help but smile as George collapsed into the nest, tearing into the food. She let him eat. She let him fall to sleep and waited for any signs that their parents would return. And she waited. Closing her eyes not once. She stared at the sky.

George slept for a few days and Clemenza realized that her fate would be taking care of not only herself but also George, helpless now. He would never fly again. She watched the sunset on the Pacific horizon each night, growing more and more hungry, more and more weak.

She had two choices. She could lie in the nest and die of starvation with her brother. Or she could hunt for food for the two of them. As she watched the Sun set that final night, she saw a strange sight: Two eagles, identical to herself. Beak entwined. Twirling through the sky. Tumbling towards the ground. But they never released their grip on each other. It was Winston and Justice. Celebrating their new freedom. Celebrating their lives together. And they were celebrating the triumph of raising two chicks to the point that they could raise themselves. It was a celebration dance. A dance of commitment to each other.

The sight both inspired and depressed Clemenza. She knew that because of her brother's disability, she would never be able to share that embrace in the sky. She would never find a mate. Her child was her brother. She would feed him and care for him until they both died.

The next day she took flight, scouring the ground for simple prey. She had been in the sky for the day and was about to call it quits when she came across a large farm, with captured animals. Ducks. And though it pained her to take such simple prey, she had to. If she didn't both she and George would die. She hovered above the ground until she found a weakling. Small enough for her to carry back home, she swooped, capturing the small animal in her talons, penetrating its flesh, killing it nearly on contact.

Back at the nest, George ate the raw flesh of the duckling. Clemenza broke the prey down into small pieces, just as her mother did for her. She let George eat the small pieces from her mouth. She ate whatever he could not. She settled to sleep that night, almost full, still awaiting the hunger that the next day would bring.

The farm seemed heaven sent. The weaklings were easy to spot, easy prey. They could only run so far from Clemenza's grasp until she caught and devoured them. She would carry them back to the nest, exhausted and knowing that once she returned, more work would call for her. The nest was in terrible need of repair. She would have to shred the meat for George again.

That evening, she searched around the nest for trouble spots. Once she settled in, she spoke to George. It was a talk that hadn't occurred since the day their parents left. They watched the sun set together, George's head propped against the wall of the nest. They both felt the heaviness of their eyes, beginning to close.

"I was there once. On the Sun." Clemenza wanted to share her past life with George. "I was a part of the Northern Lights. Have you ever seen them? They are beautiful. I danced that night with the most talented dancer that has ever existed. Aurora was her name."

George raised his head to speak. "I was some kind of bacteria on Mircronia, an ancient planet, far, far away. The planet was suffering, and species were dying. No one had made it far enough to civilization and the kind of life that Earth has. I thought I could make it. I thought I could make life happen for Mircronia. But I failed. A meteor hit the planet and I died shortly after. I wanted to make this work, too." He lowered his head back to the comfort of the nest. "I heard that the bald Eagle was nearing extinction. I wanted to help."

Clemenza nodded her head as she began to understand where her brother's determination and stubbornness came from. "I will help you, George. I will save us."

They watched the sun set until it disappeared. That night, a strong storm hit the coast and rattled the already unstable nest in its branches. The trees around them sighed. They needed the rain. And yet it was the rain that would nearly kill both Clemenza and George. The wind that they used to glide through the air tore twigs from their places, unraveling the nest.

Clemenza spent the next day repairing the damages from the storm. But it was difficult to maneuver around George. She had to lift him a few times to mend holes around him. With each lift, George's body hurt more. Clemenza flew late in the day to the farm for food.

On the porch of the farmhouse, she spotted an older man. He was staring at her. And his presence felt so familiar to Clemenza. How terrible she felt for taking and killing his livestock once she saw his face. But she had to in order to survive.

Flying back, she watched as the man watched her in the sky. She could feel his stare long after she left the farm. When she got back to the nest she began shredding meat for George. The nest was almost completely repaired. George was moving around that day. He was weaving whatever space he could to make the nest more stable. She told him of the farmer.

"I feel like I know him. His face, his stare, so familiar to me."

"You are romanticizing a great danger. He was watching you kill his stock. That's how he feeds his family, too. Don't be stupid. Stay away from him." George was being protective. But he knew the danger that Clemenza was in.

But the farm was the easiest source of food for her. She didn't have the time nor the patience to stalk her prey for days. She had to feed two grown adults. She returned daily.

On her final flight, she came to the farm near dusk. And the farmer, this time, was out in the field, holding a big stick. He was watching her. She felt the presence of danger, but didn't let it overcome her. She felt she knew him. That he was good. He would be good to her. He would understand.

As she swooped to pick up a small duckling, she felt a pop in her wing. Soon she was spiraling to the ground, but not like her parents. She was alone in this spiral, and she was celebrating nothing. Not love, not family. She thudded to the ground and felt the Earth pounding. He was running to her. For good intentions? Perhaps to save her! She could hear the man breathing hard as he reached her. He reached into his pocket and pulled out a small device that sprayed a chemical into his lungs that allowed him to take deeper, fuller breathes.

"Christopher!" Clemenza shouted. It was he, the boy with asthma! He was coming to rescue her just as she rescued him that night years ago. He was a man now. An old man. Dressed in overalls and an old plaid shirt. Covered in dry dirt. He took another puff from his inhaler.

His eyes were hollow now. He held the rifle at his side, not recognizing her, or ever really knowing her. Clemenza saw a tired man before her. The lines around his eyes and mouth told a tale of a hard life. His parents died early. He never married. He moved west to buy and farm his own land, never allowing himself to become dependant on anyone or anything, knowing that they could be taken away from him at any minute. And here was this bird before him. Not just any bird, but a Bald Eagle, stealing his livestock. Killing the animals that he called family.

He raised the rifle, knowing well that it was illegal to kill the bird.

But no one would ever know.

He buried her in a shallow grave on his farm so that no one would ever find her, taking frequent puffs from the inhaler, never knowing that he not only killed one bald eagle, but two that day.

And then she was back in line, waiting with all of the others around her to pick her next life with God. Clemenza was angry for the first time. So angry that she spoke to no one around her. Like a teenager, she replied to questions with one words answers and annoyance. She was impatient. She needed to see Him now.

In her head, she compiled a list of questions for God. Why did Christopher kill her? Didn't he know that she had saved him? That she dedicated her first life to him? Did George live? Where was he now? She wanted to be with him again. She wanted to apologize to George. He told her not to go back to that farm. And for that matter where was Marilyn and Aurora and Solare and Sally, from the beginning? Would she ever see them again?

As she neared the office and those big gates, she turned her head impatiently to the side and stared right into the eyes of an Angel. He wasn't playing any music, like most. He was watching Clemenza so intently. She tried to brush it off, and did, because she found her mind clearing and all of her questions were answered in the Angel's voice. She watched him as he spoke but his lips never moved.

Christopher never knew her. He never will, unless they were to meet in another life in a different way. She would never know what life he chose or how long he would live, until and if she became an Angel, or if God decided to answer her questions in the end. George died days later of starvation. He was in line, like her. She would only see everyone if she met them in another life, or in heaven in the end, if she chose and they chose to live in God's Tenth Life Retirement Community.

The Angel's voice, while soothing and knowing, only hurt Clemenza more. She wanted to be something that didn't feel.

As she approached God's gates, she prepared for the questions that He would ask her.

"I learned that you never really know anyone, and that they never really know you." She was still so hurt and so angry. Not just with God, but with everything. It just all seemed so unfair. He was the wind this time. A light breeze that grew stronger when He spoke.

"Clemenza. I know you think you are angry, but you are hurt above all else. I can't control everything that happens. Since I can't, I have given you nine lives. Nine lives to correct mistakes and make things right. Now, tell me. What have you learned during your third life?"

"I learned that sometimes it hurts to feel, and that feeling isn't necessarily the best feeling. I would rather not feel. I don't want to feel pain or hunger. Mostly, I learned that I couldn't control someone else's destiny. I tried to save George as if I had some sort of power. I guess I got a little hotheaded after my dancing career."

God accepted her lesson with a simple nod and sad smile as Clemenza told Him that she wanted to be a tree in her next life.

"Because trees don't feel."

Life Four

Tree

Clemenza's next life would begin on the floor of the
Amazonian forest. Not naturally. She was
methodically placed a few feet apart from another of her
kind. From there, she would be cared for everyday. She
would never have to search for food. She would never have
to care for anyone, including herself. She was provided for.

She felt herself as a seed at first. Waiting patiently
for the right conditions. She began to grown quickly. The
soil was rich in nutrients and she absorbed everything
around her, spreading herself downward, getting a firm grip
into the soil around her, spreading downward, sideways,
and upward. This was unlike anything she had ever
experienced. She was truly alone for some period of time.

She rested her mind during this time, still thinking about her past life, how she felt betrayed by Christopher. How she let George die. How she felt so guilty that George died alone, just waiting forever for her to return to that same nest that they were born in. She wanted to tell him that she was sorry, that she didn't mean for it to happen. And now she knew that the only way for her to find him was to continue living each life, searching for him always.

As Clemenza grounded her new body in the rich soils, she gradually made her way upward, growing stronger with each day. She wanted to see the light; she had enough time to think over her past life. She was ready for her new one now. Pushing through the soil, she slowly poked her head through the top surface, taking in its nutrients, feeding her ever-growing body. This was going to be a slow life, and she was grateful for it. She wasn't yet ready for the work that was required of any other life.

Days later, she finally had her first peek at her new surroundings. Feeling her body, she realized that she had nowhere to move. She could move up and out, but never over there, or through the sky, or catching the wind to fly. She felt like she was always stretching. To her right and left were trees just like her, poking their heads up at the same rate, so uniform, so lined, so rowed. From above, from the sky, Clemenza imagined the grid that she was now a part of. Her new home was very organized.

No one was speaking yet, though occasionally a human worker would walk past, staring at each plant. Judging for perfection. And sometimes there were other species that entered her view. A few worms passed, an ant, speaking so quickly that Clemenza decided that even if she were an ant she wouldn't understand the language. She was lonely. She arched her back every time a human walked past her, hoping for some sort of affection. She had no family. No mother, no father, no George. When she started missing the family she had, she thought of the grief that it brought her, forcing her to believe that she had made the right decision.

Time crept very slowly. But Clemenza felt herself growing stronger and larger every day. She started growing bark around her body, protecting her delicate insides, like a human ribcage. Waxy leaves sprouted from her limbs, now she could feel the air. She was becoming a tree. And not just any tree. She carried latex inside of her. She was a Rubber Tree, and realized that she was on a plantation that exported millions of gallons of latex everyday. She was a part of something huge. She produced something that someone else wanted and needed. Part of her would make products for humans. Part of her would create toys for children. Part of her would drive around the country.

She was identical to everyone around her. She had no outstanding qualities that separated her from the pack like on the Sun. Every tree here was being used for its sap. To her right, she began to hear chatter, and the noise grew louder and louder, until every rubber tree around her was talking, yelling. Some were screaming for help. Maybe it was their first life. They didn't understand that the few who could understand their cries were grounded in their places on this grid.

"Hey!" the tree next to her screamed for her attention. "You wanna know what's going on or are you just gonna stand there, pretending like you don't care?"

Clemenza did care. She was just deciding whether or not she wanted to get involved.

"I'm Keokee. Right, so nice to meet you, eh? I just heard what's going on and this is gonna knock you off your feet."

Clemenza was thinking that she didn't really have feet. And the feet that she had were so deeply dug into the earth that whatever was supposed to knock her down would have to be very strong.

Keokee sighed. "I can't believe you don't care. The next field over has older trees. And they're bleeding right now. Someone heard the cries. Apparently what these guys do is cut into our bark and bleed us for a few days. Until we are nearly dry. Then they wait a few days and come back. Cut just below the original cut and start all over again. This goes on our whole lives. What a disappointment, eh? What a life. I wanted to be something strong."

"Maybe what they are using our sap for is worth it. Maybe it will be used to create beautiful things, Keokee. And my name is Clemenza. So very nice to meet you." Clemenza clenched every part of her body. She wasn't ready for another relationship yet. But Keokee was hard to ignore. He was very persistent in getting her attention. The sarcasm was just dripping from her voice. And she felt bad. It wasn't Keokee's fault that she was miserable. It was Christopher's.

"Yeah. Well maybe you'll be the first tree they tap here. So you can tell us all how great it feels then, Clemenza. So nice to meet you, too."

And then there was silence.

It lasted for five years.

For five years Clemenza grew in her designated spot. She listened to the chatter around her. Keokee had made other friends. But no one spoke to her. She became an outcast. The only time she felt affection was when the humans came to prune her limbs. And that affection hurt. They were preparing her for her future.

This will make me tougher, she thought. The pain of the pruning took the place of the pain that she still felt from her last life. Which each trimming, she thought less of George and Christopher. She forgot the night she watched her parents embrace in the sky, twirling towards the Earth.

She grew tall and lean. The humans tended to her leaves. She received all the care that she needed. They trimmed her so that the belly of her body was bare, easier to tap. More room for more cuts.

And after all this grooming, after the pain of her past was torn from her new body, she was lonely. She was finally read to speak. She was jealous of the attention that Keokee received from the other trees. They all respected him. He became a sort of leader in a place and a life where they had nowhere to go. He held daily presentations. He spoke of how the trees could protect themselves. He spoke of a life that they could be living; wild, untamed, and free to grow in whatever direction they pleased. Untapped. Full of themselves. Not drained and dry and constantly healing. Free.

"I was free before." Clemenza cleared her throat. It had been so long since she had spoken, she barely recognized her own voice.

No one else recognized her voice either. They were all so accustomed to her not speaking; they assumed that she never would. So when she did speak, everyone turned to see where the new noise came from. She had their attention. She was back.

"I was free in my last life. I soared through the sky. I covered one hundred square miles of land each day. I had a family, too. And then I lost them." Clemenza let her emotions seep from her. "And that's why I didn't want that freedom this time. Not in this life. I wanted to be free of feeling. Free of guilt. Free of family."

Her leaves dropped, pointing to the ground. She said it.

"We are still your family, Clemenza." Keokee spoke. "Even though we aren't born from each other. We are all still here, experiencing the same things. We are family that way. We are united because we all share the same experiences. You don't have to be related to feel united. You just have to share the same experience."

72

Clemenza thought this over as her body became limp. Typically, it would start raining now. But that comfort, that release, would not come for Clemenza. The realization that she would always experience loss and grief, that she would always meet someone hit her hard. Even though she had the control over what life she would experience, she did not have control over the others, the others that would be a part of her experiences. She had no control. She thought of George, limp body in their nest, their home, and waiting for her to return with food. He had warned her. But he was not dead. His soul was just somewhere else, just as she was. Moving on from life to life.

And feeling this, her body began to ooze. There was a deep feeling within her, but it was not emotional. It was physical. She could feel her insides moving, roaring, begging to be released. She felt as if her insides would split her body, the movement was so strong.

Keokee watched as Clemenza arched her limbs, attempting to stretch the stirrings of her body out.

"I feel that, too, Clemenza. There is no way to stop it. Soon we will see what we are made of. The humans will be here. They will tap us. They will make us bleed. They know we are ready." Keokee stretched his limbs just like

Clemenza, trying to crack out the feeling, the sap that was moving through their bodies.

Just like Keokee had said, the humans came. The very next day, as if the humans had heard the whole conversation that had occurred the day before, the tapping began. The humans came in groups this time. Not the singular man that would occasionally come along to check on their progress. They came with knives and large buckets to collect the precious insides of these precious trees.

The carving started early in the morning, just as the sun was rising .The men were inspecting each tree in Clemenza's view, in her little grid. They checked the tree leaves, their bark. The first cut was made into a tree that was further down the grid, next to the grid that the trees had acquired all of the gossip from before. And then the yelling began.

In some cultures, the men will cut the younger men, scarring them for life, scarring their backs, their faces, their chests, their legs. All to make the young men look like an animal that they fear or worship. And this cutting was not unlike the cutting of these cultures. It was a high cut, but not too deep, curving down the side at a diagonal angle to encourage the latex to drip into the large bucket. The cut is wide and the sap oozes from the trees' inside.

From here the sap can become anything.

The first tree was screaming for God, and the others thought how silly it was. God could do nothing to stop this. He could hear the cries, sure, but the only on who could stop the cries were the ones who could either see it or feel it themselves.

As soon as the sap started to drip from the first screaming tree, which was now quiet, recovering from his wounds, letting himself bleed, the human who made the original cut said something to the others, which everyone knew meant "They are ready. Cut them now."

Knowing what was going to happen for some time now, Clemenza was quite prepared. As the man grabbed her body and began to cut, she thought of George. She thought of George lying in the nest, waiting for her, she thought of her parents twirling through the sky, beaks entwined, she thought of Marilyn watching that last performance of the Northern Lights, she thought of Aurora, committing herself to her last dance, her precision, her grace, her beauty, she thought of Christopher, aiming his gun right at her, not knowing that she had saved his life not so long ago. She thought of Sally, turning to say that he wanted to be a human for all of his last lives. And she thought of herself, how she had pitied herself. How she had allowed herself to fall into such a deep sorrow. And then she was reminded of Marilyn's sorrow, how only the beauty of the Northern Lights seemed to calm her from her troubled past.

And then, just as her sap began to ooze from her body, she remembered her dance. She practiced the movement in her mind, the graceful movements, the powerful music blasting through her head, the sharp turns, and the perfection that was demanded of her.

She produced more sap than any other tree in her grid that day. And to Clemenza, it was a way of releasing her self-pity, her remorse, and her painful memories of the past. They were only painful because she was making them that way. She had reached a new level of life. She was now aware of her own power.

Each time the trees were tapped, the moaning and complaining could be heard for miles. But they would bear this pain for nearly twenty years. Some of them had died early, some sort of worm or insect infestation. But most survived the test. The question was, where would they go from here?

Keokee told stories of giant Rubber Trees in the jungle, growing tall and proud, with wide canopies of leaves reaching towards the sky. He said that it was possible to be replanted. They weren't too large and were no longer producing the sap that the humans desired, so it only seemed right to be replanted back in the jungle, free of everything, free to grow for hundreds of years.

But others weren't as optimistic. And they had every reason not to be.

A few days after the trees stopped producing sap a noise that they had never heard before roared through the jungle floor. Three quick roars, to start up the engine, and then... the final cuts began. They were shredded. They were to be shredded and pounded and pressed. Paper. Another human need. There just wasn't one part of them that went to waste. Clemenza was blended in with everyone. Millions of pieces of her original body were everywhere. But her soul remained in one tiny piece, which was pressed and pressed and then finally bleached, which really burned.

Now she was paper. And being shipped somewhere. Europe maybe, or America. No one was with her now. Either their souls had been shredded or they existed now far apart from Clemenza. But she was on a shelf in a tidy office.

"You gonna use this paper, Larry? I'm all out. I've got something, finally."

A voice from below her.

And now she was being held and carried. Across the room. Down a flight of stairs. And into a cafeteria. Pressed tightly underneath the arms of a man who had a use for her. She could live forever if he had something good. She waited patiently as he carried her back up the stairs and into his office. The man then sighed as he threw her into a bag. He was mumbling, names, places, who knows, Clemenza couldn't understand.

That evening, he pulled her out of the bag and placed a piece of her into a machine and began to type: *A Little Green: A Novel By Richard Sleeson. Chapter One. The Awakening of Sally. On the day that Sally was born, she had faith in all that she saw. She saw kindness in flowers, insects, amazement in sounds and faces. She was pure.*

A few moments passed before the typing began again. And then the typing continued throughout the night. Richard was flying through his fictional chapters. Living his characters, breathing them. He came home from work rushed, made coffee, even said hello to his old typewriter. And Clemenza just sat. The massage of the keys felt great after everything that she had gone through. And if he actually sold the book, she could stay this way forever. No one destroyed books, right?

The day that he finished the novel, he kissed Clemenza, and if she had blood she would have blushed. It was her first kiss. He screamed something to the woman he lived with. She rarely entered the room.

"Rhonda! I'm finished! I'm finally finished. Come here and read this will ya! Just read a few chapters. Tell me what cha think."

Rhonda entered the room and took a sip of what was not coffee, but something much, much stronger, and sighed.

"Is this the book that you wrote about this Sally woman that you refuse to tell me about?"

This is when Clemenza screamed, but to herself, of course. No one could hear her. There wasn't another soul that could hear her. It was Sally! He was the writer that had been massaging her this whole time. Oh! How talented he looked and smart and inspired leaning over this little typewriter over the past few months.

"I told you Rhonda, she's not real, just fiction, remember?"

"More like some fantasy that you won't tell me about. You know what Richard? I'm sorry that I don't make you happy. I'm sorry that you have to create fictional mistresses to get through your day. I'm so, so sorry that I'm not enough for you," Rhonda snorted.

And with one swift movement of her arms, which was very *un*graceful, she tossed Richard's (well, Sally's) masterpiece into the fire. And, because Clemenza was the masterpiece, she was now engulfed in flames. But she wasn't uncomfortable. She had, after all, lived on the Sun. She danced on the Sun. She went peacefully, but sad for Sally. Sad for Sally because he had one copy of his masterpiece that was written on Clemenza and his wife had just callously tossed her into the fire.

Back in line, she was anxious. She was finally ready for the next life.

She looked nervously around her, recognizing no one, but secretly searching for any familiar face. Although she was sad for Sally, she was much more comfortable with the events that had occurred in her last life. She was okay with moving on, with living. She didn't want to be stuck in the same spot like Marilyn was, that just wasn't for her.

When the Angels called her name to step into the office, God was dressed like never before. This time he was wearing an old worn maroon sweater and dirtied khakis and small glasses that were pushed to the tip of his nose. He was holding papers, which probably said nothing, just going with the image of God as a writer or professor, which was what was in Clemenza's mind at that moment.

He peered down his nose at Clemenza, looking up from the blank pages, and said, "You look much better, Clemenza. It looks as if your last life was chosen well. Come on, you know the deal, lesson learned and whatnot."

After a deep breath Clemenza said, "Well, I want to apologize for my misery the last time I was here. I realized that no matter what happens in life, the best parts are the beings that you share the moments with, no matter what happens in the end. I will always have these memories, and it is up to me whether I make the memories pleasant or unpleasant. And I realized even more that I couldn't control everything. And. I am ready to be a human."

God tried to appear to be surprised, because that was how Clemenza imagined Him being, but he wasn't.

"I think you're ready, too, Clemenza." God was smiling. "But remember a few things, before you choose. You won't know me. Humans are completely free of the memory of past lives and heaven. I made it that way. So you can be more productive. You'll have the heart and the mind and the intelligence and the means to accomplish anything your heart desires. I wanted humans to be free. You know, if you don't know that you have lives left, you make the most of the one life that you think you have."

Clemenza was fully aware of this and she was ready. "I'm ready. I'm ready to be a human."

Life Five

Human

On the day that Clemenza was born a human, she awoke to the same feeling she did when she was an eagle. Inside of something else. But this something else was different. She was very warm and very well nourished. But she didn't know anything else. Just as God had said, she knew nothing. So each day that she spent here, she would learn something new and some things all over again.

She swam and kicked, treasuring each moment in her mother's womb. She was always cared for. Just as she needed to be at this time. And as the months passed on, she grew weary of her scenery and the organs around her began to expel her from the body of her mother. And just like that, she was born.

They named her Zara Louise McCourt. Zara, because her mother briefly studied Hebrew in college and thought it was a beautiful name, and Louise after her grandmother. Zara was the first and only child that her parents, Anne and Jack McCourt, would have. So she was their pride and joy. Every moment of every day was spent with the baby. And the neighbors came to visit and gawk and stare at how identical Zara and Anne appeared.

"She has your gorgeous green eyes!"

"And that smile! That crooked little smile that you have... who would've thought that two would share that smile!"

All of the banter made Zara laugh. She was a very happy and giddy child. She took her first steps earlier than any other child around and her first word was "ish." Jack was a fisherman for a growing business in Washington and he believed that she was trying to say "fish." But Anne believed that Zara was trying to say "kiss" because she was such a romantic. Zara's first word would be something that the couple would debate for three years, but only because they wanted the word to be something dear to them, when in fact, Zara only said "ish."

What Zara would later try to forget were the nights that her mother would sing her a lullaby to sleep, or read from one of her favorite novels. It wasn't the words that she tried to forget; it was her mother's voice, tender and loving and always so calm and soothing. Zara would try to forget that voice, and would also try to make her own voice different from that. Anything to help her father recover, Zara would do.

She was only four when they received the news. Her mother had just returned from a day at the doctor's office, a trip that Zara wanted to share with her mother, but she would not allow it. Instead, she spent that day with her father on his boat. It was the first day that she spent with her father at work. She stood in awe at the magnificent beauty of the Pacific Ocean. She felt the sea on her face, whipping through her long red locks of hair, completely tangled. Her mother would spend hours combing it out that night. Perhaps even taking out her frustrations from the news that she had received on Zara's hair.

But what Zara would most remember from that day, was her first sight of a terrific animal. A beast in the waters. Flowing freely in the waves. Coming up for air, and also coming up, in Zara's four-year-old mind, to take another peak at her.

"It's a humpback whale, little Zara," her father had said.

Her obsession would begin that day, perhaps to replace the news.

"I have cancer." Anne said it matter-of-factly. Her green eyes full of tears. Her head held high to protect her family and herself from the pain that each one of them would endure from this day on. Her hair looked beautiful that night at dinner. It was glossy and tied loosely at the nape of her neck, her long neck, or Zara's long neck. The two were the same. Zara's hair was still recovering from her day at sea.

Jack looked at Anne like he never had before, walking over to her, at dinner, placing his head in her lap and crying. His sobbing caused the tears that were in Anne's eyes to cascade down her face. Dripping over Jack. Zara thought that if her mother's tears were magic, that they could cure him of his sadness. But in the end, it turned out that there was no cure for his sadness or her cancer. Zara, normally full of questions, never asked any that day.

Her playfulness and humor disappeared as she morphed into a new Zara: responsible. Caretaker. Adult by Five. While she never would ask her father how her mother died, she discovered the answers for herself. She would bring books home from the high school library. She taught herself to read with her mother's voice. With each page that she read, she could hear the way that her mother would pronounce the word, or end the sentence. Answer the question.

She spent a few weekend days with her father on his boat, always searching for the whale that she had seen on the day that changed her life. Sometimes, her father couldn't look at her. She looked too much like Anne. Everyone said it. Phrases like "spittin' image" and "ghostly resemblance" stung Zara as if her mother's death were an open wound and the words were the water from the sea. Just flowing from the mouths of strangers who had no idea how hard it was for Jack to look at his own daughter and how difficult it was for Zara to look into her father's eyes when he looked into hers. He could only see Anne. And Jack tried to see his daughter for who she was, part of him and Anne, but his memory of Anne simply would not fade.

Each day passed, neither Zara nor Jack saying anything about Anne's death, about her passing away. No one said a word about the empty chair at the kitchen table, or the empty love seat in the living room where Anne would read, or the dying garden in the backyard where Anne would plant beautiful flowers in the spring, or the empty side of the bed where Anne once slept, or the towel that still hung from the rack in the bathroom where Anne once showered, or the basket of laundry full of clothes that Anne once wore. They spoke not of the empty refrigerator, the house that never since that day filled with the smells of fresh pies and cookies, the conversations that had suddenly stopped, the questions that were never asked, or the book that laid like death on the coffee table in the living room, marked where Anne had left it.

Zara continued to grow and continued to resemble her mother. By age seven, she was washing her father's clothes, preparing dinner, humming the songs that her mother would hum as she attempted to bake the pies that her mother once made. She cleaned the house and took care of her father. She did well in school, finished her homework before her father came home, and became a homemaker and full-time student at the age of eight.

By age nine, she had mastered her mother's pumpkin pie recipe and was starting to add her own ingredients to perfect the pie. At age ten, she revived the garden that lay dormant for five years. The flowers were blooming and full, free of weeds. She was meticulous and obsessive; every moment of everyday was spent trying to bring her mother back. The house began to smell like it did when Anne was alive. Spices in the kitchen air, fragrant flowers in the garden. Fresh linens and clean clothes, clean countertops and everything in its place.

By ten and six months, she had, by all means, replaced her mother's absence. Her hair, growing softer, was the mirror image of her mother's locks. Her stance both soft and strong, a quality of appearance that she thought only her mother could perfect. But her eyes, the emerald green that so many had commented on when she was younger, longed for something more. They were empty of passion. They were void of feeling. After all that she had accomplished, her mother was still dead. And somehow, when her mother died, her father seemed to have died with her.

At eleven, Zara was through with her attempts at reviving her mother's presence in the house, the community. She was through with attempting to fill the silence in her house with the smells of cinnamon and vanilla and roses and orchids.

Jack left for work early, hours before Zara would wake for school, preparing herself for classes and the nonexistent friendships that she would tell Jack about when he came home. But she wouldn't go to school today. At seven o'clock, she tiptoed down the stairs and sat with a straight back on the love seat that had remained vacant for years. Easing herself into comfort, she slowly allowed her back to touch the backrest of the couch that only her mother had rested on before. This was her mother's place. Lying back comfortably, she reached for the telephone on the end table beside her. This was where her mother would talk for hours to neighbors, friends, and family. She dialed the school.

"Washington Heights Middle School, how may I help you?" the receptionist was warm, but probably only from the gallons of coffee that Zara had witnessed her drinking throughout the day.

"Hello, Miss Winters, its Zara. I won't be in to school today. I might have the flu." Zara was a familiar face in the office. Not because of misbehavior. She was a familiar face for lack of a better place to go. While the other kids were off running around during lunchtime and homeroom and study hall and gym class, Zara sat in the office. She helped Miss Winters make photocopies and sometimes helped with the morning announcements. She made coffee for the office in the morning. She had no place else to go. All of the other girls her age were boy crazy, writing letters and chasing the boys around the school. Zara felt that these acts were a waste of time. She wanted to be productive, and ultimately, she wanted to get out of the school as soon as possible. She wanted to get away from the faces that knew her mother had died. She wanted to get away from the thought of her mother dying.

Zara knew that Miss Winters would not doubt an illness. After all, this was the first day of school that she had missed in years. She hung up after Miss Winters wished her well and insisted that she didn't need any help, that she would be fine, just a flu, she'd be in tomorrow. And she would be, she just had a few things that she needed to do for herself.

Lifting her body from the sofa, she walked into the kitchen and began to sharpen one of her father's paring knives. Back and forth through the sharpener, she worked diligently until the blade was sharp enough. Zara walked through the living room and into the garage, grabbed a few pieces of kindling and one log, and newspaper. She crunched up yesterday's newspaper, which no one ever read, her mother's subscription never cancelled, placing it beneath the shelf in the fireplace. The kindling was placed on top.

Grabbing a giant match from the mantle, Zara then watched as her fire came to life. Burning through the newspaper, orange flames licking the kindling above, she waited until the fire grew, and then placed a single log on top. Taking the paring knife, freshly sharpened, over to her mother's sofa, she tore through the fabric, forcing the internal stuffing to come out. She placed the stuffing in the fire, and then placed the fabric in the fire. While this was burning, and only the frame of the sofa remained, she walked into the garage again and grabbed her father's axe. In the living room, she chopped up the frame of the sofa, and then slowly placed this into the fire. Throwing it all in at once, while satisfying, would put the fire out.

Now it was incredibly hot in the house, and though Zara was sweating through her pajamas, she grabbed her mother's book, tearing out page by page, she watched the words burning, melting in the flames, becoming one with the sofa, with the fabric, with the frame, with the stuffing, all disintegrated and making their way to heaven, to be with her mother.

She still had one more task to complete before her father came home. She walked up the stairway into her father's room and sat down at her mother's vanity, paring knife still in hand. Staring at herself in the mirror, she saw her mother. Her mother's eyes, her mother's smile, her mother's hair. Taking a long red lock of hair, she lightly sawed the blade back and forth across the lock until it fell limp in her hand. A few deeps breaths later, she gazed at her reflection in the mirror and for the first time in her life, she saw Zara.

Of course her father was startled when he returned from work. Zara was new to him. She had prepared dinner, and just as he was about to sit down, he paused. Walking over to Zara, he cupped her face in his hands, pulled her to his chest, and just whispered two words: *I'm sorry*.

He never asked her what had happened to the couch and the book and her hair. It was another one of those questions that was out there, but would never be answered.

Jack did warm up to Zara after that day, the second day that would mark their lives. He continued to take her on weekend fishing trips and she would sometimes bring schoolwork, sometimes bring a sketchpad, and sometimes she would just search the sea for the whale that she had seen before. And then the third day that marked Zara's life came. She was on the boat with her father when she saw it. It couldn't be the same one, could it? But there it was, right in front of them, just as it was before, with the same markings, and the same eye on Zara.

From here on, Zara took on a new obsession. She took advanced biology courses, sketched images of the whale in art class, wrote stories about it in English class, and when she was at home, she continued her research. She told Jack that she wanted to become a marine biologist, and he did the best that he could to save up enough money to send her off to whatever college she wished to attend.

By the end of Zara's senior year in high school, she had achieved much. She was valedictorian of her class, she was offered a generous scholarship to a college with a phenomenal reputation in the field of marine biology, and she remained true to herself. She had formed a sort of bandage over her soul to recover from the loss of her mother. She let no one in. The bandage was waterproof in that it repelled tears. She hadn't cried in years. She didn't have the time.

Her obsession continued in college. At the age of nineteen, when most girls had posters of pop stars on their dormitory walls, Zara had her sketches of the whale. Her roommate, Alicia, was a typical freshman college girl. Alicia pledged a sorority, was unsure of her major, and spent her days plotting to get the star quarterback to notice her. She had long hair, like Zara used to, and used her beauty to get what she wanted. Zara requested a single room her sophomore year.

She spent her days in the library and until the next day that would mark her life, she spoke only in class and occasionally when she came home from school to her father. This day would both begin and end in the library, because Zara was always there. She was searching for a rare paper from an unknown author on the possible communication of humpback whales and was growing exhausted. She would have to ask for help.

Walking up to the front desk in the library, she approached the student helper who was filing her nails. The helper looked Zara up and down, and then pointed to another student who was shelving books in the corner. As she neared the young man, she recognized him from her classes. His name was Liam and he frequently participated in classroom discussions with ease. Zara remembered admiring his confidence.

"I need help." How else to say it? She hadn't participated in a normal conversation with anyone for years, maybe ever.

Liam stopped shelving the books, again looked Zara up and down. "Are you okay?"

Did she say it wrong? "Um, yeah, I mean, no, I just need help, like I'm fine physically, I just am searching for something and I can't find it and I just need help." She was fiddling with her shirtsleeves. For the first time, self-conscious of the way she looked. Her shirt was too big and her jeans were too long and beginning to fray. And she was even conscious of her socks. Her socks were probably the same size as her father's big fisherman socks. She recalled the day when she did her laundry with Alicia and watched as Alicia delicately folded her tiny pretty socks. Her entire pile was the same size as one of Zara's cotton fisherman socks. And it was okay until now.

Liam smiled. "Trust me. I can find anything here. And if we don't have it here, I'll find it someplace else." He walked over to the front desk and Zara noticed that his jeans were fraying, too. But it looked different on him. "Just give me your name and number and I'll call you when I get it."

Zara did, and then she ran back to her single room to change and shower and maybe put on something new. But she didn't have anything new. So she grabbed a nice clean white button up shirt and left the top two, no the top three, buttons undone. She couldn't do anything with her hair. It was too short. She had kept it short from the time when she first cut it. She put in a pair of pearl earrings that her father had given her for graduating high school. Liam didn't call that night.

But he called the next morning at 5am. He said he had been searching for the paper all night, never slept, and finally found it in a library in California. He had it rushed to their campus and would she join him for coffee to celebrate that afternoon. Zara said yes and immediately took the bus to the mall. Was this a date? She didn't know. But she needed to update her appearance just in case. The mall didn't open until 10, which she later found out. She read a book while she waited for the mall to open.

In the department store, Zara was lost. These are the things that a mother teaches her daughter. She never heard a "Oh! Honey! Green looks great on you!" or a "Never wear red with your hair color." She asked for help everywhere she went. The women in the department store were ecstatic when a make over was proposed. They helped her with her eyes and her hair and her makeup. They made her feel comfortable. They showed her what a beauty she was. And they gave her some confidence. She left the department store with a new wardrobe and a new attitude. And her first crush.

Liam was late for coffee. He said that he was waiting for the paper to arrive.

"What's so great about this paper, Zara? I mean, we know that all animals have some way of communicating with each other." Liam casually sipped his coffee and jerked his head around the cafe, greeting other students, introducing others to Zara.

She explained her obsession to him and where it came from, looking at him through her newly mascaraed eyelashes. "It all started when I was four and I saw the whale for the first time."

Liam appeared to be listening. At least Zara hoped that he was. She was pouring her heart out. She told him everything. She told him about the fire she made, about her hair, about how she burned the book. "You know, back then, I really thought that by burning her things, that I was sending them to heaven to be with her. I wanted her to have them in heaven. So that she was comfortable. It's amazing how we develop these ideas at such a young age. How imaginative!"

Liam cleared his throat. "Maybe she did get the sofa and the book. And even your hair. Maybe she has them with her right now."

After that day, after that fire, Zara didn't really realize it, but she lost her faith. That bandage that she had made for her soul didn't let anything in, even God. She told Liam this and he seemed shocked. "You mean that you believe in God?" She never really talked to anyone about religion before.

"Of course I do. I'm a theology major. That would be like being an English major and hating to read, or burning books." He winked when he said it and slid the paper over to Zara. "This was fun, but I gotta get going. I'll see you soon, kay?"

So it wasn't a date. And she had poured out everything. Maybe it was because she hadn't really spoken to anyone for so long, she had so much to say. But she got her paper. She headed back to her room and read it over and over again, and it helped her to make her next move. She decided to take an internship. The program would allow her to study marine life with the animals, the next semester, back in Washington. She was about to phone her father to tell him her plans, when the phone rang first.

She was hoping it was Liam again.

But it wasn't. And here is another marker of her life.

It was Miss Winters, from her high school office, and there had been a tragedy. Her father was knocked off the boat and she didn't want to go into the gruesome details and she was so sorry and was there anything she could do. And Zara said no. The bandage bounced the news right back.

"Have him cremated, like my mother was. And then spread their ashes together in the garden in the backyard." She was stoic. Miss Winters whispered that they were together now, in heaven, and watching her from heaven, and Zara thought of how ridiculous she sounded. The mere thought that they were together again, and not actually ashes, was crazy to her. "And where exactly is this heaven, Miss Winters?" And then Miss Winters stopped her polite sympathies, she said she would do as Zara requested, and the phone call ended awkwardly.

Zara looked at herself in her tiny compact mirror that she had just purchased early during the day while she was being made over. Her father would never get to see the new Zara. For each moment of her life she had experienced pain, and now she was void of pain, just like her house was void of love after her mother died. She was void of anything, all at once in control and yet completely out of control, faithless, and determined only in her obsession.

And now, thinking of nothing, she made her way over to the library. But not for whale communication research. She knew that Liam would be working. And she knew what she needed at that moment, and that was for someone to hold her, to help to put the bandage on, make sure that it was tight enough, just to the point of allowing circulation, yet keeping a tingling feeling so that she would know that she was still alive. Her feet were pounding on the sidewalk. She had forgotten her shoes, but she didn't even realize that yet. Not now.

Bursting through the old library doors, she walked aisle by aisle until she found him. Her hair was wild. On fire almost, lit by the fluorescent lights of the library. Barefoot and ignited by some sort of passion, she flung her body into Liam's, planting her lips firmly on his, where did she learn this? She would wonder tomorrow. Zara was now, and her target was Liam, and he graciously accepted her, dragging her tiny body into a small study cove. She wrapped her arms around his neck as he lifted her onto the wooden table that was meant for studying and Liam studied Zara, her eyes filling, the waves of green. They were empty for so long. And the pain of the moment was covered; she used it as a releasing for the losses that she had endured over the years, the kids that made fun of her in school. It felt just like that first cut that she made into her mother's sofa.

Bodies shaking, hands trembling, she was now a woman.

"I love you, Zara." But nothing. The questions were never answered.

She would think of him occasionally as the years passed. She never spoke to him after that day. She didn't want to give him a chance to ruin that moment. She didn't want to give herself a chance to ruin that moment. She spent her days on a boat now. Just as her father did. But sometimes she went into the water. Armed with high-tech equipment, she spent her days off the coast of Hawaii, plunging into the warm currents, recording the sounds of her obsession. She was a professional. She was highly respected in her field. Her thesis on the sounds of the whales, their communication, her theories, were read by biologists all over the nation. She spoke about marine life for the National Geographic Channel. Some say that the media accepted her so widely and openly for her looks. But it was her unwavering dedication.

She had no family to tend to. The whales were her family. She began tagging and naming them. Watched them make families. First came Clara, and then afterwards she followed the lives of Clara's children, and grandchildren. They were always together.

There was only one who knew what Zara did underneath the rushing tides, the swells of the ocean, when she recorded her new family's song. And that was God. He saw it all. She danced to the songs. Not a day of professional dance lessons in her human life, and here she was underwater, dancing to the symphony of the male whales, calling for their loves, a professional.

When she thought of Liam, she never thought of what her life would have been like had she answered his calls, submitted to his persistence. Because she never imagined what her life would have been life if her mother hadn't died, and her father. She only thought of them now. In the present. Her mother and father's ashes lying together in the garden, Liam probably married, a loving husband. Everyone moved on.

At fifty, Zara was still active in her obsession. She received a call from a colleague. There was a dead male humpback beached on the shores of Washington, and would she want to make an appearance for the dismantling of the animal. Her colleagues wanted to preserve the skeleton for display in a museum, unbelievably the first of its kind. The task would be difficult to witness, let alone smell, and Zara only hoped that it wasn't a whale she knew.

She flew to Washington that night, packing nothing. Only a few books and her Beethoven CD, which she always listened to on flights. When she arrived, the smell was overwhelming. Full grown men were puking their guts out onto the shore and blood was everywhere. It was Lunar, the dead whale. He was Clara's first son. A passing boat had injured him, his body brought to shore by the strong currents and tides that had plagued the area for nearly a month. He was enormous. The size of a ship and lying on his side as men hacked into his dead body.

Zara remembered a warning from somewhere, a story. A story of a man in New Zealand who attempted to transport the body of a dead humpback when suddenly the gases that were still inside of the whale's dead body expelled from his body, over turning the man's boat and flooding the sea with blood and guts.

Wanting to share the story, Zara headed down the rocky coast, step by step, as the smell grew stronger. And just as she was opening her mouth to share the story, a strange percussion from inside of Lunar's body sounded across the shore. The men looked at each other quizzically, then continued with their investigations. One more rumble and Zara was thrown to the ground, covered in the blood of Lunar. And still. Not a movement, not a sound.

The medical examiner claimed she died of shock. Eyes wide open. And the tragedy of the McCourt family had finally come to its end.

Clemenza was in line again, and still speechless. She remembered having strong feelings about God and His nonexistence, and yet here she was, back in line, waiting to see Him and share her lessons. How quickly she had forgotten her past lives, and the lessons she learned there. She felt terrible for being such a loner, and obsessing over an animal that she could later become.

"Before you even say it Clemenza, you don't have to apologize." He was now just a mass of blue, perhaps the sea. Maybe the sea was Zara's God. "You did very well despite your circumstances. But I know you wanted to have children. Many humans are faithless, but more aren't. Somehow, through all of their tragedies, they still find time to believe, and forget their present circumstances and see something beyond themselves. Others don't. You couldn't feel heaven, or see it, so you didn't believe. But you still found faith in something else, didn't you?"

"The whales? Their songs were beautiful."

"And in Liam. He helped you. Without him, only I know what you would have become." This was followed by an awkward silence as Clemenza waited to see if he would tell her what would have happened to her without Liam in her life, even if it were only a few days without him. But He didn't.

Clemenza shared her lesson. It was okay to ask for help. And saying this, she realized that she had already learned this, when she helped Aurora perform that night. Aurora had asked Clemenza for help that night.

God accepted her lesson, but never asked her what she wanted to become. He already knew. She wanted the answer to the question that was burning inside of her. But there was no time to prepare her for the answer.

Life Six
Children

Clemenza didn't know where or what she was when she started her sixth life. But whatever she was, there were millions of her here. Everyone was holding hands around her and there was a distinct sound that pounded throughout her new world. It was a constant pounding that felt and sounded so familiar, but from her new perspective, she couldn't quite pin the sound. Everyone else crowded around her, all connected.

"Gimme your hand!" someone yelled.

Clemenza looked up and reached out her hand, which was more like a million little hands, all deformed and unique and reaching for the unique hand that would hold her back. Her hand was somewhat like the limbs she possessed when she was a tree, but she was far simpler than a tree now. She grasped onto the hands above her, but they weren't the right fit, so they floated away and Clemenza distinctly heard someone say, "*Did you see her hands? What's wrong with them?*"

Only a minute into her new life she realized that it wasn't going to be easy. What was she? She never told God what she wanted to become. He must have assumed from her thoughts. She wanted to tell him that she wanted to have children of her own her next life. How could she have a child like this? The others already thought that there was something wrong with her. She couldn't even touch anyone else around her.

Her body began to feel weak and she closed her eyes to her new world and thought of everything that she knew of her old lives. Zara came to mind. And when she thought of her life as Zara, she thought of Liam and that day in the library. Their hearts racing together. She wanted to have children with Liam. But Zara's obsessions would not allow anyone but herself to exist. If only she could go back.

Clemenza felt a strange sensation coming over her new body, like a separation, tearing her apart. Unsure of what she was, she began to feel as if her remorse over her past lives was making her physically ill. And then she paid close attention to the noise. The pounding. Ba bump. Ba bump. Ba bump. Ba bump. Slowly at first, then speeding up. And when the noise came faster, babumpbabumpbabump, everything around her was affected by it. Everything in her and everyone around her was linked directly to that noise. Slowing down now. Ba bump. Ba bump. Ba bump.

A drum. A beating drum. Constant. Supporting the life around it. As she realized what the noise was, her body tore into two. She was two now, her soul encompassing the two beings. Ba bump. Ba bump. A beating drum. A heart.

"I'm a cell." She thought back to her simple biology courses that Zara took in college. The basic structure of life. The feeling made her at once realize how primitive and limited she was in this new life. A cell's major function was to divide.

Now four, now eight, now sixteen. Her body grew. Separate cells, but one mass. The mother of a million children. The mother of herself. She tried to speak to the other cells around her, but they no longer spoke the same language. Knowing that only the same creatures spoke the same language, Clemenza knew that she was somehow different from the other cells that she understood only a few minutes ago. At least it felt like minutes. There was no way to determine time here. Just the beating of that heart. But what kind of body did that heart support? That would be the only was that she could determine time.

Clemenza attempted to move, and by judging her size compared to her surroundings, she was still small enough to have a look around her new environment. The best way to find out what being she was housed in what to get into the bloodstream. She was still multiplying, but was at such an early part of her life that she was just small enough to make her way around.

But moving around proved to be more difficult than she had imagined. Her sense of time was so offbeat. The heart was pounding more quickly now, at least to Clemenza. She was growing more and more quickly. And her body, now thousands of cells, was unable to hold together, and she broke into multiple parts and lay on the walls of her new home.

Because her body was torn now, her mass was broken; Clemenza was still able to receive information from each cell. The places where she lay were broken into lobes. The beating of the heart was so close, so loud. She must be in the lungs. Human lungs.

Wishing that she could speak to God directly, she attempted to count the cells that were a part of the mass of her being. Two hundred and fifty-six here, five hundred and twelve there. What were the ideas that were running through her mind when she last saw God? And that was when Clemenza remembered the question that had haunted her during her whole life as Zara: *What killed my mother?* Cancer. Clemenza was cancer. Lung cancer. Putting everything together now. God was answering the question that had tormented Zara and ruled her life as a human. *What killed my mother?* Cancer.

Having never killed a being before, with the exception of food when she was an eagle, Clemenza did not want to be here. She continued counting. Sixty-five-thousand-five-hundred-thirty-six here. One-hundred-thirty-one-thousand-seventy-two there. One million-forty-eight-thousand-five-hundred-seventy-six total. Math now. Just basic. Thinking of Zara's courses, cancer cells divide every eighteen hours, which meant that she had already divided twenty times, making her only fifteen days old. She was still very curable, but still growing rapidly. And in the lungs!

Clemenza started paying attention to everything now. Everything gave her clues to what was about to happen. She determined that the being she was inside was a smoker. And it was because of his smoking that she came to life. He created the deformity. One cell was all it took. One cell that never knew when to stop multiplying. One cell that was different from all the others. One cell that carried its deformity on to all of its children. One undetected cell. Clemenza.

The immune system must kick in soon. The t-helper cell acted as a conductor of the immune system. This cell would send for help by acting as the conductor, the composer of the immune system. Clemenza continued to divide. Autoantibodies began to flood the human's system. All it would take was a simple blood test to catch the cancerous Clemenza in time. She had no control. It wasn't in her to stop. All that she could do was hope and pray that God would not allow her to kill again. She let George die. She just came to peace with her past lives. She wanted another chance to do well. She wanted to make things better.

And at the same time, she understood. She understood how her mother died. She knew what killed her mother. She understood the basics. She now understood that her mother's death was not her fault. The cancer was not controllable. She was not responsible. The only way that her mother would have lived was if a soul that cared was living inside of her body and thinking of the environment that it was destroying and not itself.

How old was she now? Close to seventeen million cells.

Clemenza continued counting. All that she did was count. As her cells continued to divide, she never rested. She constantly divided and continuously counted. She wondered how long it could last. How long could she last here without killing the very being that made it possible for her to live?

Then she stopped counting. Not because she lost track. She stopped because there was nothing more to count. She was fully-grown. Finally. Still cancer. Still abnormal. The human must have started chemotherapy to stop her cells from dividing. At last! Rest! She closed her eyes and allowed her mind to drift off, no longer worrying about numbers and division. She thought only of heaven.

For the first time in all of her lives, Clemenza felt her soul leaving her life behind. She was lifted from the body that she had once attacked and stared directly into the face of an older woman that she would have surely killed. She smiled at her. And the woman smiled back.

Once in heaven, Clemenza already knew her path. She wanted to become a human again to make up for all of her wrongs. She wanted to be a good person, a citizen, a model for others. The older woman's smile made her think that life isn't all that bad.

In a moment she was back to the gates, back to God. He had no physical presence this time, just the sound of the beating heart. Ba bump. Ba bump. Ba bump. And Clemenza understood every word He said.

"I learned that despite being something that is bad, you could still turn it around. I learned that I had to die in order to let something that was bigger than me live. That woman was my environment, and regardless how much either of us fought, we would both have died if I had continued to take over her body. It was better for one of us to go."

One day, all of her lives would be revealed to her. Their connections were divinely planned. Some questions were best left unanswered, because all would be answered in the end. She would be sent back to Earth as a human for round two.

Life Seven
Human

Soaring through the universe to her new life, Clemenza tried to remember everything that was important to her, everything that would help her get through another human life. She was ready for this. This time, she would make a difference. She would make it better this time. She would be better.

But none of the preparations mattered as she entered her next life. Her mind was stripped away of memories of God and heaven, past lives and friends, advice and emotions. All was blank. *Tabula Rasa.* One could debate whether God had instilled this theory to John Locke, who believed in God without evidence, without proof, without human experience. But why would God instill ideas in some and not others? The questions are answered in the end.

Warm and inside of her new mother, Clemenza fed off of the nutrients that allowed her body to grow. While she grew, she was comforted by one sound that pulsated throughout her body and the body that she was growing inside. The ba bump ba bump of her heart beating with her mother's. The two shared the same body and their hearts beat as one. In her mother's womb, Clemenza was in stereo with her mother's heart.

The birth of Clemenza was difficult for her mother. The head was too big, stuck between her mother's pelvic bones and flooded with the numbness of painkillers. Her first breathe, inhaling her own bile. But she made it. Emergency cesarean. Life would be different for her this time. Trouble from the start and no memory of her first day in heaven when Sally said to her: *There is no such thing as gender*.

Born Ian Robert Filmore, Clemenza took on a new gender. But there was no other gender that she knew. She only knew that she was Ian as the doctor proclaimed: *A surprisingly healthy boy, Ms. Filmore!* as he placed a crying Ian on the chest of his mother. Their hearts began to beat together again.

"My little Ian!" his mother said as she stroked the head of her newborn child. "You will be a strong, healthy, handsome man. My little man." And as she whispered lovely thoughts of what their life would be like into Ian's tiny ear, she started humming and then the humming turned to singing. The most beautiful voice! His mother's. Sweet and full of whispers and highs and lows. She sang to her new baby boy and Ian quickly took in each word, each note, and each scent of new.

Once at home, Ian absorbed his surroundings. Flashes of light, warm reds, soft yellows, and the blues of his mother's eyes. Each sound, the hum of his mother's voice, the pots and pans in the kitchen, the furnace, was an adventure in his imagination, a quest to be solved. A gigantic jigsaw puzzle with the house as the outer pieces, and Ian as all of the more difficult to place inner pieces.

As the days passed, Ian heard strange noises. Slamming doors and screams from his mother at an unknown voice on the phone. But more pleasant was his mother's singing. Every time she saw Ian, she would sing the same song. And Ian was happy. Ian learned the smells of his surroundings, the bittersweet scent of milk on his own breath, his sense of smell linked directly to his sense of taste. He could feel his own body growing, his senses improving.

There were certain sounds that Ian learned to block out from his mind altogether. The sounds of his mother yelling, for one. As the yelling became more and more frequent, he learned that these sounds made him feel uncomfortable, so he simply blocked them out, replacing the discomfort with the comfort of his toys and the pleasant sounds that he could make around him.

As he grew, he became more dependent on his ability to simply leave an unpleasant situation. Once, while playing with his toys in the middle of the living room floor, his mother began to yell into the phone again. Hearing her sobs and cries, Ian gathered his toys to leave the room and was in such a rush to leave the discomfort that he ran right into his bedroom door. The door was normally opened. His mother closed it to keep her screams muffled from the kitchen.

Ian cried as the pain from the impact caused him to drop his toys to the floor. He could hear his mother's footsteps running to the bedroom and then stop.

"What happened, honey?" Her voice was soft and worried.

"I want to go to my room!" Ian yelled, feeling around for his toys on the floor.

Silence now. All that he heard was the sound of his mother's breath and the beating of her heart, rapid now, as if it were about to explode.

"Your toys are in front of you, Ian. Can't you see them?"

Ian turned around and began to feel for the toys around him. Nothing. Just blurs and flashes and the sobbing gasps for air from his mother.

The doctor told Ian's mother that it was likely that Ian could see some movement from birth, but that even these flashes and blurs of light that he saw would eventually disappear completely. The doctor, who smelled like Listerine and Lysol, said that Ian would have to learn to use his other senses in order to have a life of his own. At five years old, Ian would have to learn routines, smells, sounds, and rely on the feeling of touch. He would never see his mother's face, the blues of her eyes.

There were sounds that he grew accustomed to. Ian fell asleep every night to the sobs he learned to block out. His mother's cries and response to dealing with the hard fact that no matter how she looked at Ian, he could never see her back. She cried at each thought of Ian, in a special school, Ian, never learning to drive a car, Ian, at graduation, smiling into a faceless, nameless crowd as he receives his diploma. She cried for herself, too. She cried about fighting with Ian's father, whom Ian would probably never meet. She cried about keeping Ian after she broke things off with his father. Perhaps this was God's way of punishing her, a punishment for being so careless and selfish. But it wasn't fair that Ian, helpless, fatherless, and innocent, had to deal with the consequences of her past.

None of this bothered Ian because he knew no better. He wouldn't miss the flashes of light because they always startled him. And he would never be disappointed in appearances. Instead of focusing on all of his senses, he focused on his sense of hearing. After the doctor's visit, Ian's and his mother rearranged the house so that it would better fit Ian. No door was ever to be closed, no cabinet ever left ajar. Ian felt around the newly arranged house and memorized each position, the tilt of the chairs, the angle of the coffee table, the rough texture of the carpet in the living room compared to the smooth linoleum tile in the kitchen and bathroom. He tapped each countertop, each wall, each mirror, and each windowpane. And to Ian, each piece of his house made a differently distinct and beautiful sound to him.

He could tell what pots his mother was grabbing from the cabinets by their sound. He knew where his mother was by each creek in the floorboards. This was a beautiful house to Ian. He knew and heard every inch.

Enrolled in a school for children who would face society from a different angle, Ian excelled in all of his courses. Socially, he met and kept new friends. He was always the first to be picked for special assignments and Valentine's Day crushes.

"You know, you have your father's charm, Ian." She let it slip one day.

Ian was ten at the time and had neglected to bring up the subject of his father because he knew from the nights of crying and yelling into the phone that this was a subject that she didn't want to talk about. He was trying to be considerate to protect her. But now was a good a time as any to find some truth.

"What was his name, mum?" They were sitting at the kitchen table, Ian tapping at the table with different utensils and his mother flipping through a magazine. And he felt her head go down, nearer the tabletop. And she took in a heavy breath.

"Michael." Another deep breathe. "I met him at a party in college. He was the son of a senator. A courteous, charming man." Another deep breathe and Ian felt her smile. "And a real prick."

The word stuck in Ian's mind for days. Prick. Prick. Prick. It was such a pointy word. He used it in class to describe a classmate that he liked and quickly learned that prick was not another word for charming.

For his twelfth birthday, Ian requested a voice recorder to record the sounds that he was obsessed with in and around the house. For days his mother found him in the corners of each room, slamming doors and cabinets, putting the lid down on the toilet seat, opening the refrigerator, and sliding the mail out of the mailbox.

By Christmas his obsession had grown still. He needed now another recorder, so that he could make an album using the first recorder.

"Whatever for, Ian? What do you plan on doing with two recorders?"

Ian responded that he was making a symphony of the house. The noises that he heard were all coming together now into one recording. And that New Year's Eve, the entire Filmore family sat captivated around the coffee table as Ian's recording was played. He heard his mother stifle a tear as the sound that she knew well, the phone slamming, played over and over, but giggled as the sound of the toilet seat being put down echoed throughout the room.

"At least he put it down." She laughed.

What was more impressive was the second recording that Ian made from the noises in his classroom. His teacher observed a raw talent for breaking down sounds into their most basic form, and fitting them into place with other noises. She recommended taking him to a music studio because of his sensitivity to sound.

Ian's mother contemplated this for a while. Three months to be exact. And each day, Ian persisted. She smiled as she watched him record noises around the house.

"Listen to how different the penny sounds when it is dropped into the pan from how it sounds when I drop it on top of the pan." Ian was obsessed. He couldn't stop with the noises. He had every intention of showing his mother that he had a talent, a knack for placing certain sounds together to make a new kind of music. He was a genius. Couldn't she see it?

On the final day of the hold out, Ian was in the bathroom recording the leaky faucet. She hated that noise. And here was Ian, ear next to the drip; recorder in hand, thinking it was something more. Something beautiful.

"You can go." And though she wanted Ian to think that she was giving in to his persistence, he knew that she saw something there. She saw something more than guilt.

Of course she accompanied Ian to the studio. How else would he get along? For all of his life after his impairment was discovered, she worried. Would he feel that step? Would he break his fall? Would he sense that door? Would others torment him? She was his protector, she felt. Who else was there to protect him? She must be all.

She leaned into Ian and braced his arm as they started up the stairs. But he rejected her touch.

"You don't have to do it, Ma. I've got it. I'm fine without you."

And though Ian meant for his words to be reassuring, he had no idea that his mother had no one else but him. If he didn't need her, who did? But he was nearly a teenager. He wanted to be on his own. He asked her to stay outside of the studio; he was ready to be alone. He could handle this. This was his. But he felt her presence the whole time as if she snuck in and watched him, never saying a word, never taking a breath. She needed that. She watched him as he interacted with others, how at home he was here. How natural this was for him. He was in command. He took her hand down the stairs after the session was over. And he listened to her breathing, shallow, holding back the tears that would fall that night when she didn't have to deal with her own reflection of sadness.

He chose a college far away from home. He knew it would hurt her. But it was best for both of them. They were dependent on each other. She thought that he needed her in order live, to make it through the day. And he thought that she needed him to make it through the nights, when the cries started. If no one were there in the morning to stop her tears, would they ever stop? He found a college that was far away from every inch that he knew. Until now his life was one of routine. It had to be. Unknown territories could mean danger.

Ian's departure date was filled with his mother's tears. She cried during the car ride. She cried when they popped the trunk of the car in front of his new home. She cried when they climbed the stairs and Ian stumbled over the first step. She screamed.

"Your first step here! This was a terrible idea, Ian. I will never forgive myself for allowing this. Come home. Let's go back now." She sniffed her tears away and put up a strong front, but the front was merely a front, and behind the wall the fort was soft and sad.

"I'm fine. Just relax. Let's just get into the room. That's the real first step."

Ian's room was small, which was good. It was easier for him to memorize. And Ian's room was small, which was bad, more bits of furniture that he could run into, bump his head, lay crying to help on the floor for days before anyone would hear. No matter what, his mother would think of the negative. She didn't want him to be here. Everything was terrible. Until she met Cassidy, the girl from the room further down the hall.

Cassidy was tall and thin, with dark wavy hair that hit her waist. She was walking through the halls, peeking into rooms, when she caught Ian's mother's eye. She seemed innocent, but caring and still had an air of confidence about her. She smiled, almost embarrassingly as she caught the gaze back to her. Ian's mother leapt to the door to catch her before someone else did.

After introductions and learning that Cassidy grew up in a smaller town, and Cassidy learning that Ian was blind, the caring side of her took charge and the friendship began. Now it was safe for mother to leave.

Cassidy did take care of Ian in school, but so did Ian's roommate, Davis. Davis was loud and opinionated. He was also well connected. He supplied the entire college town with all the drugs it would ever need, and a secret stash in case it wanted more later on. Davis claimed that they were all family, everyone he met, because they all shared the same experience together. College.

But what Davis had that Ian craved was not knowledge. It was an anti-anxiety drug. He only took it in the safety of his own room, but he never knew where it would take him. And he wasn't addicted to the drug itself, just the feeling that it gave him, the power, and the power of sight. During the nights when he would take his pill, Ian reverted back to his early childhood. Sure, he started at eighteen years old in a dirty dorm room, but he ended in the living room, by the coffee table with his toys, listening to his mother on the phone, and watching the lights, those flashing lights. It would start with a flicker here, and a burst there, and before her knew it, the whole room would be covered in colors, colors that he couldn't describe but could taste, colors that he didn't know the name of, and his mother's eyes. Her eyes! Ian did know one color. It was blue. Her eyes!

Cassidy would hang around for Ian when he took the pills. She made sure he didn't leave the room. She knew it made him happy. He had managed to pick up another protector.

On the night that Ian told Cassidy that he loved her, he saw her, he swore he saw her clearly for the first time. And Cassidy cried, never having the heart to tell Ian that she had dyed her hair, that her eyes were green, that he was wrong. She would be whatever he wanted her to be. She loved him, too. She loved him from the first time she saw him. Once, she happened to be in the music building at the same time that Ian's class met, and she peeked through the door just to get a glimpse of him. There was Ian, in front of the class, playing the music that he had made from the sounds of the college campus. He was so happy.

Cassidy cried then, too. After the class was over, Cassidy wanted to see him, and ran up, nearly to him. But he was walking, holding arms, with another girl. She had a beautiful laugh. And they turned the corner, missing Cassidy completely, until Ian turned abruptly and called.

"Cassidy?"

But she was already gone. Yes, she did love him.

Ian and Cassidy were only sophomores when they found out she was pregnant. They were home for Christmas break. Ian sat on the sofa, his mouth ajar. Cassidy sat with her head in his lap. Ian's mother was in the kitchen and dropped the pot of boiling pasta to the floor.

"That's a beautiful sound," Ian said.

"I want to keep it," Cassidy said.

They both dropped out of school and moved home. Cassidy took up residence in Ian's room and Ian found new noises to record. He started sending out his tapes. Someone else had to appreciate what he had done. He stayed awake all night, recording the sounds of Cassidy sleeping, the crickets, anything, everything was music and beautiful.

Davis would visit once a month and supply Ian with the drug that opened his senses. The recordings became more bizarre. And for some reason, it was the bizarreness that made him. He would go for days without showering, perfecting his tapes, perfecting the sounds that he made. He reverted back to his childhood completely, with two mothers now instead of one.

The day that Ian found out his music was accepted by a big label, that he would make a living discovering sounds, his mother drove them to the hospital. Cassidy was a beautiful mother, everyone said. She was glowing, they said.

They named her Heart and when Ian held her for the first time, he sang the song that his mother always sang to him. *The first time ever I saw your face.*

Cassidy cried and his mother cried, because he would never see her face. Her green eyes. But Ian smiled, because he could feel her beauty. He didn't need anyone to tell him what she looked like because he could feel her beauty. He vowed to be the father he never had and married Cassidy the next week.

Heart took her first steps when Ian was in Africa recording. She called out "Dada" when he was in Hawaii recording the ocean. He was in London when Cassidy took the training wheels off of Heart's bike and rode down the street and back, Ian's mother clapping in the front yard. When she started junior high and won junior homecoming court, Ian was in India. And when Heart found out she was accepted to Harvard, Ian was at home, in the basement, perfecting his recordings, door closed.

Cassidy left Ian when Heart left her for college. Ian bought a loft in the city and called her when he needed help. He called her when he was too drunk to realize he missed twenty years of his life. He called her when he felt guilty for not feeling guilty for what he had done. Cassidy thanked God these nights for caller ID.

Until the night Ian stopped making sounds, he never realized what he had missed. He lay with his feet up on his expensive sofa, and fell asleep to the most basic of all noises, the beating heart. Until now, he had never realized that he missed her; he never realized where her name came from. And then his new obsession began.

The Heart series was the most popular of all of his albums. Colleagues recognized him. People came to him for advice. They came to him for his special ears that heard music where music had never existed before. He wanted to record other hearts beating, and the label paid for him to travel abroad, capturing the pounding hearts of animals. It was in Africa that he decided that the beating hearts of tranquilized animals were not good enough. It was the pills that led him into the wild, with no Cassidy to protect him, to capture the sound of a wild animal's heart.

The recording was found later, but still before parts of his body were. It was phenomenal and eerie, capturing the moments of Ian's death, in the throws of a lion's jaw. But he never said a word. He didn't want to ruin the recording.

In heaven, Clemenza was numb. She finally had a child, a human child. How selfish she was! She wanted to go back, to see Heart, to see Cassidy. She never saw anything, just held onto the memories of the voices that she loved. Despite her actions as Ian, she knew that she loved Heart and Cassidy. Clemenza had to show this to God. She had to let Him know that she needed to go back. She wanted to make things right. She needed to see them.

"Well. That was a bit different, Clemenza. How do you feel?" God was a kaleidoscope of color this time. His office was flooded with the most beautiful colors that existed nowhere but here. This office was the only place that could hold this kind of beauty. The colors twisted and formed indistinct images, meant to be anything that she wanted them to be.

He already knew how she felt.

"I don't usually let anyone go back, Clemenza. This is breaking a few rules. What is your life if you can't learn from mistakes? You can't always go back."

"But I don't want to go back for me! I want to go back for Heart. Just make me anything so that I can help her, or even see her, for a second! Please!"

God is not unkind. Clemenza was going back through the warped tunnel, heading straight for Earth. She would try to mend the mess she had made. She would try to be a better father. She had no idea what kind of life God would give her. He was granting her a special favor. He was giving her a second chance. But he would give her a second chance in His own mysterious way.

Life Eight
Clemenza

Soaring through the universe was the easy part. The hard part was trying to figure out God's plans for her. She hadn't specifically chosen a life. She hadn't told Him what form she wanted to take on, what challenges she wanted to face. Or did she? Sometimes God knew more of what was going through her mind than she did.

Suddenly, she was warm again. A mammal, she must be. Wrapped up in this warm cocoon with so many others. Hungry. How many were there? One two three. Six total. Including her. Now Clemenza knew that she was a mammal that gave birth to litters. There were so many options.

Through the birthing process, Clemenza was anxious to find out what she was. Throughout all these lives, who she was remained constant, but the *what* always changed. Then she heard it. Her mother yelping. That yelp was so familiar, her mind was racing. What was she? She pushed her way closer to her official entrance to her new world and saw nothing. Panic. He wouldn't allow her to be blind again, would He?

She felt the coolness of the air on her body, her mother licking her clean, but saw nothing. She heard her brothers and sisters pawing around her, she felt them pushing away, hungry for her mother's milk. And then a human voice. How could she recognize it?

"The cutest puppies I have ever seen! Six tiny puppies!"

And Clemenza now knew what she was, where she was, and what her purpose was. He was allowing her to connect. She understood human language, English in fact. What Ian spoke, and most importantly, what Heart spoke. God was allowing her to make the connection. Now she just had to find out how she would get to Heart.

Being a puppy was by far one of the most fun lives Clemenza had ever started. She was so soft and cuddly, the human that owned her loved to pick her up and snuggle with her. She was tiny and brown and had the softest, fluffiest fur. She had four brothers and one sister. Her brothers were mostly black, some with white spots, and her sister, Lawna, was completely white. The humans called Lawna "Snowflake" and simply called her brothers "the Boys," because there was hardly any way that they could distinguish between the four of them. They called Clemenza "Brownie" which made Clemenza hungry.

Clemenza played with her brothers and snuggled with her sister. But mostly she ate. She ate everything. If a human left something on the floor, she ate it. If something was crawling near her, she ate it. If something was in Lawna's fur, she ate it. The humans, at first, scolded her for eating everything. But as their patience grew thin, they laughed. Clemenza was unstoppable.

There was no marking of days and time so Clemenza was free to do as she wished. But the time spent with her canine family made her nervous. She didn't want to get too close, knowing that once she was adopted, chances were very high that she would never see them again. She never talked to her siblings about past lives. She never asked them questions about anything. In her first few lives, all she did was question. This life was not for her. It was for Heart.

At four months old, the puppies were ready for adoption. Other humans began visiting their home. Clemenza would run to the door, anxious to see if Heart was there, waiting to adopt her. She became disappointed and snarled at guests, scaring them off from adopting the pretty brown dog. Perhaps she would have to run off and find Heart herself.

Clemenza was left with two of her brothers. Lawna was quickly adopted. The new family called her "Sugar." When the doorbell rang for the final time, Clemenza was too tired to get up. She stayed by her mother's side, but perked her ears to listen to the new human voice in the house.

"My name is Helen, this is my husband, Jordan... Our first dog."

The last three words were said in excitement, and Clemenza recognized the voice. In it she heard the same excitement as the day that Heart found out she was accepted to Harvard. She ran over to Helen and Jordan, jumping up in Helen's arms, licking her face, her curved tail wagging so fast that Jordan joked about a breeze in the room. Helen reacted affectionately as the family that raised Clemenza, or "Brownie," had never seen her respond this way to anyone.

"It was meant to be, then." Helen curled her arms around Clemenza's chest and hugged her tightly.

The car ride to her new home was excruciating. While Helen and Jordan talked about names for Clemenza, she became more and more sick in the backseat. Helen would occasionally toss her arm over the passenger seat and give Clemenza a pet to the head, but Clemenza wanted none of it then. She felt nauseous and dizzy, and finally, just a few seconds from her new home, as Jordan said, she let it all out.

"It looks like she must have swallowed a pen cap." Jordan peered at the pile of vomit in the backseat. "Look at that! Is that a pen cap, Helen? She must eat *everything*."

Helen tenderly cleaned Clemenza up while Jordan set up Clemenza's new home and all of her new things. "Of course we pick out the dog that gets carsick," she yelled from the bathroom.

Jordan walked into the bathroom to see Clemenza covered in soapsuds. "I didn't think we had a choice. She picked us, didn't she?"

Clemenza stared at Helen the whole time, letting her scrub the terrible smell away. Was she the same Heart?

Why was she going by the name of Helen? Clemenza fell asleep in Helen's lap as she dried her off.

They still hadn't decided on a name. They both agreed that "Brownie" didn't fit her.

"What about "Maniac?" Jordan was at the kitchen sink, rinsing dishes from the night before. "She eats everything. Only a maniac would eat a pen cap. What else did she eat? Oh! Last night, she ate half a roll of toilet paper."

Helen said No. No, she was not a maniac.

That night Jordan came up with the name they would choose.

"Let's name her 'Clemenza.' You know, that big guy from the 'Godfather?' That would be perfect. Cause she's tough, and like it or not, she's gonna be big if she keeps eating everything that she sees."

Helen looked down at Clemenza, who was lying in her lap. So much for the doggie bed. "Clemenza," she said.

And Clemenza looked up at her, and licked her chin.

"Looks like she likes it. Clemenza it is."

Clemenza didn't know when she would grow out of the phase of eating everything. It just felt right to her, chewing on things. The first to go was the cable cord in the bedroom, just hanging from the wall, practically calling her name. Clemenza had free reign over the house while Helen and Jordan were at work. At first, they attempted to keep her in the kitchen with a baby gate. But when Clemenza climbed the gate and brought over her toys with her, they couldn't bear to keep her locked up all day.

"She's just too cute."

Clemenza fell asleep every night in Helen's lap. She shared the bed with Jordan and Helen and she followed Helen everywhere. As soon as Helen got up in the morning, Clemenza jumped to her feet. There had to be some reason why God made her a dog that Heart would adopt. They even named her with her own name. It all just seemed too perfect.

It certainly seemed to Clemenza that she was making Helen happy. Helen took her everywhere. She went to work with her now, she took car rides (with the help of some Dramamine), and she even lay beside the tub when Helen took her nightly baths. The two were inseparable. This was how life should have been when Heart was born.

Clemenza should have been there. She missed everything. And even though she knew Heart as Helen now, there was still something missing. What it was, Clemenza could not quit put her finger, well, paw, on it.

For Christmas that first year, Clemenza could see that Helen was wrapping presents for her. She was excited for a new toy or bone and jumped up and down, trying to get a peak at what she would be opening Christmas Day. That night, she didn't sleep at all. She couldn't wait until morning. It was her first real Christmas with Heart.

When the doorbell rang, she was so excited she ran from the kitchen, where she was monitoring Helen making quiche, to the foyer, paws scratching and sliding all over the freshly oiled hardwood floors.

"I'm coming!" Helen called form the kitchen.

Clemenza pushed her nose to the door, trying to catch a sniff at whatever was behind it.

"Merry Christmas, Ma." Helen gave the woman a hug and kiss. "How was your flight?"

"Fine. I mean, terrible. Delays. I had to open my luggage and empty out everything that I worked so hard to fit in one suitcase. But other than the embarrassment of feeling like a terrorist, I mean, I seriously started to feel like one, wondering where I hid my C4, it was fine."

Clemenza stood back from the door and looked up at her. She was so beautiful. When was the last time she heard Cassidy? The last time she really listened to her? Her hair was still long, but not as long as Clemenza remembered, and her eyes bolder than she had ever imagined.

Cassidy at once took to Clemenza.

"You know, your father never wanted a dog. He said he was afraid of killing it. He said he would step on a puppy. I think he was just afraid of taking care of something else." As Cassidy spoke she curled her arms around Clemenza, just like Helen did that first day together. "I suppose my grand-dog would like to open her presents now."

Cassidy pulled a candy cane bone from her giant purse and Clemenza jumped all over her, trying to reach it.

"This dog is quite a blessing! Just look at her, Heart!"

As Cassidy said it, Clemenza looked right into Helen's eyes. This was the first time anyone in the house referred to Helen as Heart, all of the proof that Clemenza needed to know that she was in the right home. Helen's eyes were teary. The name made her sad.

"You know, Ma. You know why I couldn't bear that name. It was his name for me. It was all he cared about. Not me. It was just the name." Helen grabbed her mother's luggage and began to carry it up the stairs to the guest bedroom. "Call me Helen or honey or sugar or whatever else you want to. But don't call me something on Christmas Day that you know very well breaks my heart. No pun intended."

After the confrontation, Clemenza stuck by Helen's side. She wished that she could just tell Helen that she was sorry, that she never meant to cause her any pain. She wanted to tell her that she was a selfish man, too stuck on her own disabilities to wonder about anyone else, or take care of anyone else.

At dinner that night, Cassidy apologized to Helen as she slipped some turkey and mashed potatoes under the table for Clemenza.

"The strangest thing, though, Helen. You know, when I called you by that name, the dog just looked at you. She looked right at your face, into your eyes. Almost like it was a confirmation of something." Cassidy took a sip of her wine with her right hand and tossed a piece of bread under the table with her left.

"She understands everything we say, " Jordan spoke up, mouth full of food. "She understood sit and lay down and roll over and stay and pick which hand the treat is in from the beginning. We didn't even need to house train her. She's incredible. She really is a part of this family."

Clemenza was so happy to hear that she made someone happy; she walked over to Jordan and set the piece of bread in his lap.

Jordan giggled as he took the bread fro his lap and revealed it to the table.

"Mother! No table scraps! Jeesh, that looks like a whole piece of bread." Helen just shook her head and smiled. She was a good dog.

After Jordan received a big promotion at work, he came home happy. He threw his bag of papers onto the kitchen table and hugged Helen. "Things are going to get better for us, honey, I promise. This is a great opportunity."

Helen was crying and Clemenza knew why. She loved Jordan, and wanted him around as much as possible. This new promotion meant longer days, nights even, and sometimes a few weekends. She knew what it would turn

144

into. Jordan knew it, too. Neither one of them needed a bigger house or more money. They just needed each other. But like anyone, if you throw enough money in front of their face, they can change their priorities.

With Jordan home less, Helen became more reliant on Clemenza. She wanted Clemenza right next to her all the time. If Clemenza slept too long, Helen rushed her to the vet.

"This is normal," the vet would say. "She's just getting older. Like we all do."

After the tenth visit to the vet in one month, the vet suggested that Helen talk to a doctor about her paranoia. And he also had some unsettling news.

"This breed, Helen. Their typical, average age. What I mean is. The average age they live to is twelve. Clemenza is getting older. She's fourteen now, even that is a feat. She's just tired. Things affect her differently now."

Helen aged with Clemenza as well. If Clemenza was sleeping while she was cooking, Helen would put the cooking on hold, carry Clemenza to bed, and fall asleep with her so that she wasn't alone. She would cover Clemenza with the soft comforter and curl up with her. She would rest Clemenza on her belly as she read on the couch.

Everything made Clemenza tired. Just walking outside hurt her joints. She ached from any activity and would try to sleep through the pain. But she still felt lucky. Even though she knew that she was dying, she was grateful to have these fourteen years with Helen. She felt a sort of closure, but not completely. Something was still missing.

The day that she would die, Clemenza did not get out of bed. Not her bed. The bed that Jordan bought for her years ago went unused. She always slept in the warmth of Helen and Jordan's bed. Helen didn't get out either. Jordan stayed home from work that day. He knew. She knew. They all just sat around and waited.

In her final moments, her last few breaths, Helen stroked Clemenza's head and whispered to her and Jordan stood behind Helen and held her shoulders. "You were our baby, Clemenza. We love you so much. Thank you for all of the happiness you brought to our lives. You were the baby we could never have."

They both cried when they carried her limp body to the backyard and placed her with her toys and favorite blanket into the hole that Jordan had dug a few days earlier. Helen would place flowers at the site every week for years

146

afterwards. But on that final day, Clemenza got her answer. The reason why God made her a dog was because Helen wasn't able to have children.

Back in heaven, Clemenza felt a wave of happiness wash over her. Finally, Clemenza had a life that she felt good about. God could see and feel her happiness as she walked into the room.

"You don't feel like there is anything else you want to be, Clemenza?" He was dark now, just how everything looked for the last moments of her last life.

"I feel like I'm done. I've done everything that I have wanted to do. I finally feel like I have some closure. There is nothing that could top my last life. It was perfect. I made someone else happy, my daughter. I feel like I fixed something. What more is there?"

"There is one other option, actually. A few take it. Most are too selfish to 'waste' a life on other people." He had Clemenza's full attention now. "You could become a guardian angel. Every now and then, I come across a family or a group that needs some looking after. Once they get back on their feet, your life would end. It is actually quite a wonderful feeling."

"Can I do it? I mean, I thought that becoming an Angel was something I could do only after my nine lives were up. Isn't this like skipping a life?"

"Becoming an Angel," He said, "is a permanent position. Eternity. A guardian angel is a more limited position. It's challenging and selfless. Once the family or group you are looking after is back on the right tack, you are done."

Clemenza didn't even think about it. She was ready to help. She was ready to give back.

Life Nine
Guardian Angel

T he first thing to remember is that you can help only
one family or group of people." God appeared to
Clemenza now as a bright, blinding shot of light, always
coming from whatever direction that she was looking in. "I
will choose whom you will help. But once you are there,
you will feel the urge to help everyone, and this can't
happen. Otherwise, everything would be perfect and ideal,
and honestly, unreal. There would be no consequences. We
can't have that."

Clemenza watched as God flipped through some
sort of portfolio that only Mary Poppins could own. He
would turn to a page, pull out a list that would shoot up to
the sky, and some lists even had additional lists that popped
out on the sides. So much information.

"I know you are wondering. This is a book of all the people that need some looking after. Mistakes happen. But these people can't recover themselves. They need some guidance." God was still flipping through the book that grew larger as he spoke, just like the brochures that listed lives in the lobby of God's office. The numbers that were always growing, more people choosing lives.

"Here is a family, in Pittsburgh, Pennsylvania, in the United States. The Gordon's. Mother, Janet, is addicted to pills. The rest of the family has no idea what her weight loss is attributed to. She doesn't believe in me and knows about her husband's affairs. Paul, her husband, is an addict himself. But he is addicted to having affairs. He has never been faithful to Janet. He actually believes in me. Sometimes that happens. People who do terrible things believe in me. Weird, eh?"

"What do I do for them? I don't quite understand how to help them. It sounds to me like they just need some counseling," Clemenza said.

"I'm not finished yet. They have three kids. Two older boys. One daughter who seems to be taking after her father. Caroline is sixteen and is probably going to be pregnant any minute now." He paused as the book changed, a new list popped out. "Okay. She's pregnant now. And the boys are into drugs that are more serious than their mother's choice, and selling them, too. The kids have no belief in any higher power. Caroline does at times, but she forces herself to. No one speaks in this family. Your job will be to give them some guidance. Get them set off in the right direction. Then they will be fine. But right now, I show," again another list popped out, "that the whole family is heading for extinction."

"They don't have any lives left?" Clemenza had more questions than this.

"The things that they have done to other people, Clemenza, are terrible. I really don't think they deserve it. That is why they need your help. You are their second chance to finishing their lives up and, maybe someday, living in heaven. I want them here. So, go. Your time starts now."

Clemenza was confused as to how she was supposed to get to Earth. Every other time she left heaven some other force shot her there like a bullet. The last time she checked, she was still in the form of a fluffy brown dog. Peeking down her toes, she saw human toes, and then human hands, human legs. She felt her face with her hands just to be sure. Yes! A human face as well. You never knew up here. There was another feeling, like arms, more than two, and she flapped them, the large white wings that would point to the heavens.

Flying to Earth on her own was a feeling like none she had ever experienced. It was little effort to fly, and her wings could never tire. She did have to occasionally point herself in the right direction. Her gown matched the darkness of the universe. White gowns were reserved for permanent Angels only. Black gowns were for guardian angels. Their powers were the same. Guardian angles just had them for a shorter period of time. Clemenza felt no shame in this. She was looking forward to helping the Gordon's, though she had no idea what her first step would be. For now, there was the universe to enjoy.

Arriving at the Gordon residence, Clemenza felt her wings tuck into her gown. Should she knock at the door? No. That was absurd. They couldn't see her. They couldn't hear her. This was going to be much more difficult than she realized. She felt a pressure push through her body as she walked through the closed front door.

The house was beautiful. The foyer was grand and open, with hardwood floors, not a speck of dust. The chandelier above Clemenza shined like the blinding lights of heaven. She continued walking around the main floor, searching for any one of the Gordon's. The large kitchen, with its cozy breakfast nook that no one sat in anymore, was empty. The dining room was empty. Clemenza got the feeling that it had been empty for years. The whole floor was like a ghost town.

Clemenza began the climb up the many stairs that she assumed led to the bedrooms of the house. Although her feet were mimicking the motion of climbing stairs, no pressure was felt on her body. As she stopped moving her legs and feet, she continued up the stairway, more gliding than climbing. She could control her movement with her mind. Her body seemed to be there only for her own comfort.

Outside of the first door on the upper floor, she heard the faint sound of a girl crying. Clemenza poked her head through the door and gasped at what she heard.

"I can't do this. What am I going to do? I have the money. I'll get the abortion. Dad would kill me if he knew. I can't just drop out of school and raise a child. I am a child! And Tommy doesn't even care. He doesn't care about me. All he cares about is his fu..."

Clemenza quickly snapped her head back into the hallway. That had to be Caroline, the young girl who was pregnant. Clemenza heard every thought that was running through Caroline's mind when she put her head through Caroline's door. She sighed of relief. Finally, some ground. If she knew what everyone was thinking, she could pull it all together and get this family moving in the right direction.

The boy's room was quiet with the exception of the radio blasting, each boy fast asleep in his bed. It was early afternoon. Samuel, the oldest, was dreaming about the girl from his science class. Allen, the middle child, was dreaming of the video game he always played. His thumbs were twitching, as if he were playing in his sleep.

The master bedroom was right down the hall. Clemenza, smiling despite the circumstances, was gliding down the hall to her next room, loving the feel of moving without moving a muscle. After deducing that Paul was not at home, she followed the sound of sniffing into the master bathroom where Janet stood, all hundred pounds of her, counting her diet pills on the counter, clutching some sort of locket in her hand. It was engraved. Someone named Sophia had her name engraved on that locket that Janet was clutching and the profanities that ran through Janet's mind were endless.

Lifting herself to the house rooftop, Clemenza needed a little space to decide how she was going to handle this family. Paul walked in late. "Late night at the office" he would tell Janet. Janet wouldn't respond. She acted as if Paul never came home though they were sharing the same bed. Janet would scream at him later that night, Caroline stayed in her room, and the two boys never told anyone that they were leaving. No one except Clemenza knew that they came home at seven in the morning, just in time to get ready for school that same day.

Clemenza stayed on the roof, watching the sunrise. She asked God for help, but He didn't answer. This was something she had to do on her own. She thought about her abilities and options. She couldn't physically throw the family together and she couldn't make them love each other. Something had to happen, something that would bring them together. She had to make them appreciate each other, first. Then they could learn to love all over again.

In school that day, Clemenza watched in horror as Samuel punched another kid in the face in the boy's bathroom, Allen got so high that he fell asleep in class and didn't wake up until three class periods later, and Caroline left school as if no one would notice and took off to Tommy's house. She was driving Samuel's car there, and had intended to bring it back to the school before the day was over. Caroline listened to sad songs on the radio, sometimes singing along, sometimes crying so hard that the words that came out of her mouth were unintelligible. Her mind was still racing, thoughts of Tommy leaving her. Thoughts of her father's anger over her situation.

Clemenza watched the passing cars on the freeway, listening for any clues, anything that could help her out here. For the most part, Caroline thought only of her current situation and Tommy. Sometimes she thought about baby clothes, sometimes she imagined her and Tommy getting married. But for one second she had a flashback memory, a memory that would let Clemenza know that she was savable and that Caroline might be the source to save the whole family.

It was a childhood memory that Caroline envisioned so vividly, Clemenza thought for one moment that she was actually a part of that memory. They were all young, the kids, Caroline, Samuel and Allen, staying up late, huddled in the corner of Caroline's bedroom underneath a blanket, patiently waiting for Santa Claus to arrive. Each had a list of toys that they were hoping for in front of them and they were trying to communicate with Santa, urging him to come early this year, because they had all been very, very good. Caroline, though only in kindergarten, did very well on her ABC's and 123's and was a classroom favorite. Allen, though only in first grade, was excelling in his history and drawing pictures of times past. Samuel, though only in second grade, had mastered the art of writing in cursive and was the classroom storyteller.

It was shortly before midnight when their mother came into the room, finding them by the light of the flashlight that they had not so cleverly left on. But as a child, you assume that if you can't see anything, that you can't be seen as well. Janet threw the blanket up into the air and huddled the children into her arms.

"You have been so good this year, kids. Santa came early. In fact, he was just downstairs, and he left a letter for each one of you." Janet kept the silly grin on her face as she ran down the stairs into the living room, following the children.

There stood Paul, arm at his hip, eating the last of the cookies that the children had carefully placed by the tree for Santa. They were so worried. Caroline cried that the family didn't have a fireplace, *How would Santa get into the house?* Paul assured her that if she was good all year, that Santa always found a way to get into the houses of good boys and girls.

Paul grinned as he took the last cookie bit into his mouth, watching the kids' faces as they marveled at the tree, all of the presents, covering the living room floor. What the kids didn't know was that Paul had just received his big promotion, that soon they would have a house with a fireplace. "You guys were so good this year, Santa came a few hours early. He said that this was his first stop."

Samuel stood over the heap of presents, carefully scanning each box for his name. "Can we open them now?"

"Of course!" Janet said. And with that the kids tore into the presents, laughing, comparing toys, and having the best time of their lives. Janet and Paul were, too. They held each other tight by the tree, grinning ear to ear.

Caroline was smiling at her memory, gripping the wheel tight. Everything changed after that. There was no Santa Claus. Paul was never around. Janet started speaking to the kids with a deeper, more hateful voice. They had no idea what was going on, so the only choice they had was to separate, lock themselves in their new rooms in their new big house with the fireplace that Santa would never come down.

Clemenza felt Caroline's happiness at the thought of the childhood memory. She felt warm when Caroline thought of sitting under the blanket with her brother's, she felt the shock and excitement at learning that Santa had arrived early. She felt the love at the memory of Janet and Paul holding each other and looking over their children. This family was far from being lost. There was love there, Clemenza just had to help them find it again.

Clemenza spent the nights on the rooftop of the Gordon home, contemplating her big move to get the family to see what they were missing, get them to see what they were headed for. It would have been so much easier if she could talk to them. Only Paul believed in God, so why would they have any reason to believe in love and each other. Remembering that God told her that Caroline had faith at times, Clemenza realized now that He had given her a clue. Wings pointed up towards heaven, Clemenza was now sure that she knew the way to saving this family.

Caroline had frequent childhood flashbacks, and Clemenza was present for each one of them. She concentrated on how each memory made Caroline feel, the warmth of their home, the silly games the kids once played, the fear of losing it all. She memorized the way that Caroline felt when she had these memories and duplicated them within herself. Before too long, she was able to make herself feel Caroline's memories.

Caroline was on her way to see Tommy with Clemenza invisibly seated in the backseat. She found it easier to observe with a little distance between her and the family. Once at Tommy's, Caroline and Tommy debated about what to do with the child that was growing in Caroline's belly. Tommy insisted that Caroline get an abortion, that money wasn't an issue. And Caroline insisted that he love her and the baby. She felt that they could make it work.

Sensing Caroline's discomfort, Clemenza began to recall the good, warm memories that Caroline had unknowingly shared with her. As the fighting between Tommy and Caroline continued, Clemenza stood behind Caroline and placed her hand over Caroline's back, right behind her heart. Clemenza felt a swell of energy flow between the two of them, rendering Caroline speechless, and filling her with pleasant memories.

Finding a new strength from the unknown energy, Caroline stood facing Tommy, with her mouth ajar.

"What now, Caroline? What do you want from me?" Tommy stood, feet wide apart, ready for battle, lighting a cigarette.

"Nothing. Absolutely nothing." Mouth still open and mind racing, Caroline grabbed her car keys and walked out to her car. She settled into the seat, set both hands on the wheel, and began to pray for the first time in years.

God, please forgive me for my carelessness, for my selfishness. Please forgive me for not believing. Forgive me for taking life for granted. Guide me to a better life, a better life for me and the child growing inside of me. I want this to work. I want to make this better.

Clemenza sat beside her this time, in the passenger seat of the car, praying with Caroline. And if Caroline could see Clemenza, she would see that she was smiling. She knew that this was the first step to making this family love each other again.

Caroline pulled the car into the grocer's parking lot. Once inside the store, she walked through the baby aisle, staring at diapers, handling the different formulas and food. She touched the pacifiers and bottles with her right hand and held her belly with her left. She left the baby aisle empty-handed and headed towards the produce section.

What to make for dinner?

Clemenza was beginning to enjoy Caroline's presence more and more. She whistled the same songs that

Caroline whistled and walked with the same light gait. Caroline decided on pasta with chicken and broccoli. She even bought a package of cake mix and some crushed pineapples and cherry pie filling. She remembered her mother making the sweet and simple concoction when she was young. *Crushed pineapple under cherry pie filling, topped with yellow cake mix.* Clemenza could almost smell the sweet creation baking.

Caroline returned to an empty house and started chopping. She started to boil the water for the pasta and chopped the chicken into bite-size pieces, throwing each piece into the sizzling hot pan. She preheated the oven and layered the sweet ingredients of dessert in a pan.

Janet and the boys came home within minutes of each other. Not a word was spoken until they reached the source of the smells that wafted throughout the house.

"You need some help?" Samuel asked, but never let Caroline answer, grabbing the knife and chopping vegetables for the salad that Caroline had planned.

Allen poured the pasta into the boiling water and took on the task of cooking it until the pasta was just the perfect firmness. Janet put the dessert pan into the oven, and for the first time in years, Janet, Caroline, Samuel and

Allen sat at the kitchen table, sharing their day with each other.

It was perfect, Clemenza thought, until she realized that Paul was missing. Hesitant to leave the pleasant kitchen conversation, Clemenza spread her wings and set about finding Paul's car. He must be on the freeway by now. But headed where?

She found Paul in someone else's neighborhood, making a left here, a right there. Not quite at his intended destination: A new female co-worker's home. Clemenza slid herself into the backseat behind Paul and filled herself with the memory of that wonderful Christmas Eve, when the kids were just kids and Janet and Paul still loved each other. She waited until the feeling and emotion of the memory was strong enough to place her hand on Paul's back, just behind his heart.

Paul jolted in his seat. Never thinking and driving as if he was on autopilot, Paul pulled a dramatic U-turn, tires screeching on the tidy residential road. He nearly hit a mailbox, or two. But he was happy. Clemenza felt the tears welling in Paul's eyes as her remembered that Christmas Eve, too.

When did I let myself lose that? When did I stop loving my kids?

Although Clemenza sensed the guilt in Paul's soul, she also detected the faintest feeling of faith. Renewed.

Paul veered into their neatly landscaped cul-de-sac, hitting the driveway with such force that the trunk of his car popped open. Leaving his keys in the ignition and the car still running, Paul ran into the house, sweating now, looking fevered and relieved at the same time.

Just as Janet finished setting the table, Paul leapt into the dining room. *When was the last time he had shared dinner with his family?*

"You're home early, honey," Janet said. But there was a different tone in her voice. She wasn't angry or insinuating what they both already knew.

"I just got the feeling that I was missing something." Paul put his hand over Janet's that held the silverware that she was setting on the table. With his free hand, he touched Janet's face and put his lips to hers.

"Jeesh, I didn't know that I was interrupting." Allen backed out of the dining room and walked back into the kitchen, giving his parents a moment. "Mom and Dad are making out in there," he said as he threw himself down into the kitchen chair, plopping his feet onto the chair next to him. "I say we give them a few minutes or an hour." Allen giggled at his own joke and the thought of it.

Caroline put the finished pasta in a bowl and set it on the countertop. "Hey, do you guys remember when Allen took the training wheels off his bike?" She stuck her finger into the bowl to grab a piece of fresh broccoli.

"Yeah! He totally showed me up! Here I am, learning to ride a bike for the first time. Dad's running behind me, letting me think that I am doing it on my own. And Allen's in the garage taking a wrench to his training wheels. He rode right past me! I was so mad! Show off!" Samuel laughed and pretended to take a jab at Allen, who then pretended that he took the jab and fell to the floor.

"Let's take this food out to the table. They've had enough time and I'm starving!"

At dinner that night, they all said a prayer, thanking God for all that they had and, most importantly each other. Clemenza watched from above as Caroline shared her news and her decision with the family, but the love that was re-ignited that night wouldn't allow for any setbacks. Clemenza's wings began to flap and she knew that it was time to head back to heaven.

God's Tenth Life Retirement Community
The Answers

Instead of waiting in line, Clemenza was directly transported to God's office. The room was much bigger than it had ever appeared before and was lined with gigantic books on either side that seemed to stretch the length of the universe. Each book had a name on the outside of it. Clemenza saw that her book sat on top of a large desk that was placed in the center of the office. As she walked toward the desk, two Angels approached her.

"What you did for the Gordon family was wonderful. Welcome back."

Although Clemenza was satisfied with the new happiness of the Gordon family, she didn't feel that she was completely tot credit for it. They weren't such terrible people, they just needed to realize what they had and rekindle the love that they all once shared. That was all.

"No easy feat," said another Angel. "Two others went before you to help them and came back after years of work."

In heaven now the Angels' true faces were revealed. Before, to Clemenza, an Angel's face always appeared as a million faces, constantly changing. Clemenza came to the realization that she had reached the end of her journey and was both sad and relieved. Tired, mostly. The life of a Guardian Angel allowed for no sleep.

She waited for what seemed like an eternity, but the wait was well worth what was about to be revealed to her. Today, she would get her answers.

When God finally revealed himself, the first thought that Clemenza had was that He truly made man in his image. He was an older man with silver hair, not white. Silver, with a tin foil like glare. His beard was long and silver as well and his face showed the stress and contemplation of a man who had lived for millions and millions of years. So much weight he carried on his shoulders! His eyes were like the light of the Sun, but easy to look into. And when Clemenza looked into His eyes, she felt warmth and compassion, as if a warm, summer breeze had just passed through heaven.

He was dressed in a white robe, which blended into the ceiling and floor of His office. The book lined walls and the large wooden desk were the only items that broke up the shocking white of the room. He motioned for Clemenza to have a seat across from Him and a chair quickly appeared where Clemenza was to sit. He told her to get comfortable while he opened her file.

What can only be described as the universe's best and original PowerPoint presentation, God opened the book that contained the lives of Clemenza.

"Where do we begin but the beginning?" He said with a grin on His face. This was his favorite part of His role. The connecting-of-the-dots of lives. "Just stop me when you have a question. Actually, you don't even have to stop me. I will know when you have one. Just relax." He leaned back a bit and cocked His head to the side.

Clemenza took a deep breath to prepare for the answers to all of the questions she had regarding her past lives. First on the list was Sally.

Sally, the microorganism that Clemenza met her first time in heaven, was Richard, the writer that wrote his novel on the compressed particles of Clemenza's life as a tree. Clemenza already believed this, but hearing the truth from His own mouth was overwhelming. She felt a relief in knowing that He sometimes interlaced the lives of souls. He said to think of the universe as a gigantic woven basket that the weaver weaved with no pattern whatsoever. Every so often, you would have souls that met not only once, but sometimes three or four times, depending upon how far along in their lives they were.

Clemenza also found out that Christopher, the young boy with asthma whose life she saved when she was Oxygen, was in fact that same man who shot and killed her during her life as a bald eagle.

"But he had no idea that it was you, Clemenza." God responded directly to the emotion that Clemenza was feeling. "Remember that different species have different languages, and Christopher had no idea that you were his saving breath as a child. He saw you as a pest and a threat to his farm. Believe me, he felt terrible when he found out what happened. That was his last life. He's in the Retirement Community, now."

Next, God revealed the most amazing connection in Clemenza's lives. Aurora, the choreographer of the Northern Lights later became Miss Winters, the office assistant in the school that Clemenza attended during her first human life as Zara. Throughout her life as Zara, Clemenza was grateful for Miss Winters because Miss

Winters gave her a sort of emotional umbrella after her mother died. And even after that, Miss Winters spread the ashes of both her mother and her father in the garden in the backyard of the house that Zara grew up in. She tried to help. They had a strong bond in two lives without ever knowing of their previous life as dancers of the most spectacular show on Earth.

"Aurora is actually in her fourth life now. She headed back to the Sun. Solare was making quite a mess of things there. He's back to being her back up and she's the main show again. She's a great soul, just had a few issues with control, I guess." God continued, "And it was Miss Winters that had the cancer."

Clemenza froze. She had worked so hard to stop herself from multiplying in that human body, and there she was, eating away at the body of the one soul she was truly connected to. Miss Winters did everything she could to survive that cancer. Amazingly, until now, Clemenza had no idea that Miss Winters was a smoker.

"She would sometimes steal away from the office for a few minutes after a rough morning," Clemenza said. "I guess it all makes sense now. I'm just glad that she beat me, she beat the cancer." There was silence. "She did beat it, right?"

God smiled at Clemenza's concern. "She did beat it. But she still died younger than she should have. She couldn't quit smoking. It was stress relief for her. Funny that she never took a dance class as a human, huh?"

Clemenza didn't really see the humor, but smiled nevertheless.

"You really have quite a few connections here, Clemenza. Keokee, the loud tree in the Rubber Plantation later became Davis. Your, eh, drug-dealing friend." God's stare at Clemenza was strong enough to melt iron. "I didn't expect that from you, Clemenza, but I made an exception for it because when you came back here after your life as Ian, you wanted to make up for the life you missed. You wanted to see Heart so badly and make things right. I wanted you to succeed. I want everyone to succeed. Some just don't have the selflessness or the patience to find out how."

The final connection was not as surprising, and just like every other connection, it made perfect sense in the end. It only made sense that something that Clemenza loved and admired would make a return in a later life of hers.

"Clara, the whale that you followed as Zara, was Cassidy, your wife, Heart's mother." And with that, God closed the book.

"That was why I was so drawn to Cassidy, just like I was drawn to Clara, the whale. Mysterious. And I never saw Cassidy, just like I never really saw Clara." Clemenza took in all of the connections. They all made sense and even her perception of the universe seemed to change. Of course souls had to be re-used. The heavens were like the recycling center for souls.

Clemenza still had a few questions, but before she could finish thinking about them, God had the answers.

"Marilyn, from your life as air, is still there. She has come back here twice now. Each time, she saved an asthmatic person's life, so I have no reason not to let her go on like this, constantly sky-gazing. And as for everyone else, they have been waiting for you here. But that choice is yours. Though you have struggled throughout your lives to find yourself and be good, in the end, you became selfless, and that is what life is all about. There is no feeling like helping someone who needs helping. It seems like such an easy thing to do, but to honestly want to help others and enjoy doing it is not as easy as it seems. Some souls are too concerned with their own lives to sacrifice it for another's."

God slid a translucent piece of paper in front of Clemenza. She now had three choices. There were three boxes with three possible lives on the paper. The top read: *Check One*. She could go back to one of her previous lives, try to become an Angel, or retire from life entirely. There wasn't a particular one of her lives that she wanted to go back to, because the same characters wouldn't be there. It just wouldn't be the same. And those people, those souls, were what made her lives so phenomenal.

Clemenza was already a Guardian Angel, and though she truly enjoyed helping others, Clemenza felt a deep sense of exhaustion that was overcoming her. She checked the third box, thanked God, and began to make her way to God's Tenth Life Retirement Community. Here she would see Justice and Winston, her parents when she was a bald eagle, and Jack and Anne, her human parents from her life as Zara. She could be with Liam, her first love, from the library, again. And she would finally be able to see George, the brother that she still felt that she had abandoned in the treetops.

"Just one final question," Clemenza said as she neared the door that would lead the way to her eternal life in heaven, greeted by the souls that she loved throughout all of her lives. "What are you, God?"

God nodded his head. "What else could I be, Clemenza, to make all of this happen? The universes, the heavens, are all guided by one constant, unchanging rule." He held out his long arms with his palms facing Clemenza. "I'm a mathematician."

Clemenza smiled as it all made sense to her now. Liam had appeared by the door, holding out his hand for hers, the two of them feeling just as they did together in college. He had been waiting for her. She left God, creator of the universe and creator of the number, full of answers.

Made in the USA
Lexington, KY
01 September 2013